Special Needs, Different Abilities

Special Needs, Different Abilities

The Interactive Method for Teaching and Learning

Marjorie S. Schiering

ROWMAN & LITTLEFIELD
Lanham • Boulder • New York • London

Published by Rowman & Littlefield
An imprint of The Rowman & Littlefield Publishing Group, Inc.
4501 Forbes Boulevard, Suite 200, Lanham, Maryland 20706
www.rowman.com

6 Tinworth Street, London SE11 5AL

Copyright © 2019 by Marjorie S. Schiering

All rights reserved. No part of this book may be reproduced in any form or by any electronic or mechanical means, including information storage and retrieval systems, without written permission from the publisher, except by a reviewer who may quote passages in a review.

British Library Cataloguing in Publication Information Available

Library of Congress Cataloging-in-Publication Data

Names: Schiering, Marjorie S., 1943- author.
Title: Special needs, different abilities : the interactive method for teaching and learning / Marjorie S. Schiering.
Description: Lanham : Rowman & Littlefield, [2019] | Includes bibliographical references.
Identifiers: LCCN 2019011053 (print) | LCCN 2019020237 (ebook) | ISBN 9781475849950 (electronic) | ISBN 9781475849936 (cloth : alk. paper) | ISBN 9781475849943 (pbk. : alk. paper)
Subjects: LCSH: Children with disabilities—Education. | Learning disabled children—Education. | Special education—Study and teaching. | Learning, Psychology of.
Classification: LCC LC4015 (ebook) | LCC LC4015 .S34 2019 (print) | DDC 371.9—dc23
LC record available at https://lccn.loc.gov/2019011053

Contents

Foreword	vii
Preface	ix
Prelude	xiii
Acknowledgments	xv
Introduction	xix

Part I: Information Gathering and Distribution Concerning Special Needs and Different Ability Learners — 1

1. Reaching/Teaching Varied Learners — 3
2. Response to Intervention, Individualized Education Program, Classroom Organization — 9
3. Individual Processing Style and Social Cognition — 13
4. The Interactive Method: Student Engagement and Self-Efficacy — 21
5. Memories and Interactive Learning Techniques — 39
6. Interactive Learning Technique Pluses, Leadership Building, and Alternative Means of Assessments — 47
7. The Reciprocity of Thinking — 55
8. The Cognitive Collective: Thinking and Feeling — 67
9. Definition and Examples of Reciprocal Thinking Phases' Skills — 75

Part II: Different Ways of Teaching, Personal Commentaries, and the Author's Closing Thoughts — 81

10. IM's Self-Reliance and the "How-To" of Teaching Thinking — 83

11 Objectives of the Interactive Method and Its Components	93
12 Two Personal Perspectives Addressing Special Education	103
13 Commentary and Personal Experience: Teaching and "Being" Special Needs	113
14 Author's Summative Sharing: Classroom Comfort Zone	121
References	125
About the Author	131

Foreword

Upon first meeting Dr. Marjorie Schiering, one is initially struck by her personable character and later fascinated by her depth of knowledge pertaining to the field of education. As Marjorie likes to say, "No put downs . . . only lift ups." Words. Our words are powerful indicators of who we are and what we believe. Marjorie, more than any other person we know, lives this idea. The words of this text are a true testament to the woman she is, how she has chosen to live her life, and the ways in which she teaches her undergraduate and graduate college students.

A prolific storyteller at heart, Marjorie often uses this innate skill to engage learners and to form connections with students and colleagues. These stories of her and her colleagues celebrate our differences in abilities, needs, attributes, instruction, and thinking.

This book begins with discussion of varied learners and concludes with parent and/or teacher narratives that propel both students and teachers to a place that fosters learning. Subsequently, voices of parents, teacher candidates, and veteran teachers provide multiple perspectives to help the reader understand learning differences. Educators meeting the needs of individual learners through differentiation of instruction is the overarching theme of this text.

Five decades worth of instructional ideas, theories, and personal stories merged to become this book and its companion book, which values each individual as a unique learner and teacher of any subject. "Differentiation advises teachers to respond to student needs with invitation, investment, opportunity, persistence, and reflection" (Sousa & Tomlinson, 2018, p. 35).

Dr. Schiering's writing addresses the aforementioned components while also allowing readers to be children at heart through the integration of play. Vygotskians believe didactic play provides a zone of proximal development "of a number of unique skills and act as a complement to make-believe play" (Bodrova & Leong, 2007, p. 137). Play is learning in disguise, and the wide variety of game-based activities in the companion to this book provide educators with a multitude of instructional practices that can be easily adapted to meet the needs of learners.

In the aforementioned companion book, teachers have the ability to alter these differentiated activities for their own unique set of students. There is the added bonus of illustrations to accompany the step-by-step instructions that bring the activity to life for the reader! This book and the one that follows feature a section of personal narratives. These provide an array of stories from a range of viewpoints: educators, parents, and lastly, Marjorie herself. These form a conglomerate of meaningful sharing from experiential learning and teaching those with special needs and/or different abilities. The ultimate storyteller, Dr. Schiering has an innate ability to combine current research and theory with personal narrative to address a variety of topics, including the teaching of thinking.

This first book concludes with Dr. Schiering's thoughts on this work of art. Her actions model and exude the passionate message demonstrated in these two books by stating: *We all matter!* What better way can we convey this message to our students than to differentiate instruction to meet their needs? Adapting lessons and activities exemplifies this belief and sends this pivotal message to fellow educators, parents and guardians, and most importantly, to our students.

—Madeline Craig, EdD, and Patricia N. Eckardt, PhD, professors in the Division of Education at Molloy College in Rockville Centre, New York

Preface

Perhaps you should first know that this book and its companion are written in the fashion of having a conversation with you, the reader. You will be asked questions in hopes you'll reflect on these and share your thoughts and feelings with others. You are now asked to look around you if you're in a classroom, and if not, to think of at least seven people you know. Recall their facial and general physical features to your mind. Do they look the same? Probably not. So imagine this concept: If we don't look the same, we well may not learn the same way. Madeline Hunter (1989) exemplified this idea when she stated, "Expecting all children the same age to learn from the same material is like expecting all children the same age to wear the same size clothing."

Just as we are dissimilar in appearance, so too are our instructional (academic) abilities and needs regarding learning different. Along with this are the varieties of *social cognition* individuals experience. Things such as room design; the ability to talk with others; comfort zones; chances to work alone or in partnerships, groups, and teams; and adherence to the idea of emotional safety in the classroom with lift-up statements all can have an influence on each individual's learning.

This book addresses the topic of learners with special needs. Learners with special needs require instruction using nontraditional instructional methodologies, as traditional modalities often don't accommodate all students with different abilities. The companion book includes an overview of terms and concepts involving thinking, the acronyms used in this book, and then assignments and their requirements along with a multitude of activities for primarily activity-based differentiated instruction. This Interactive Method (IM) includes the author's 1995 Interactive Book Report (IBR) with its self-corrective educational games, activity-based learning centers (ABLCs), and project/performance-based learning (P/PBL) techniques.

Both books recognize that students with special needs impact on educational resources and special education classes are part of that. The connection between special needs and special education is one of the key factors for teacher preparation programs at colleges and universities over the past decades, so much so that one may receive a degree in special education.

Practices to ensure classroom learning, as school curricula focus on active involvement with P/PBL work by student learners, has become vital. This is not exclusive to special needs students, but very inclusive with the three-tier Response to Intervention (RTI) program and Individualized Education Programs (IEPs) where differentiation morphs into adaptation- or accommodation-style lessons. For clarification, adaptation/accommodation-style teaching refers to one child, one problem, and one solution for remediation regarding learning difficulties. Since the adaptation is considered for one child, this differs from differentiation, which commonly is for two to several students or for a small group arrangement.

Just as important as groupings (or lack thereof) are the means for teaching and learning through critical and creative thinking. Sometimes the latter is considered less important than the former, but, with loss of this thinking the child becomes clustered in a more traditional learning environment in which individuality is minimized. This environment does not allow for the implementation of different abilities and different ways, which I and the contributors to these books support with respect to a hands-on learning methodology.

Here's one reason for the idea of providing differentiated types of teaching/learning instruction: There is a wide expanse of comprehension levels and abilities among student learners. Sometimes these are unexplored. While some student learners might be successful at learning by listening, others may need visual stimulation and/or tactile and kinesthetic (whole-body) involvement when learning. These are known as *perceptual preferences* or *modalities*. The commonplace feeding of information to students by talking "at" them or "to" them has been modified, suggesting and providing reason for the use of interactive instructional resources and a hands-on approach to teaching and learning.

Then again, adapting lessons to how one processes information and best learns may be reliant on the following factors, as stated by Dunn and Dunn, (1978–2008) in doctoral candidate courses and their books on learning styles: time of day when instruction is provided, students emotional components, a formal or informal setting, and psychological factors as well.

Other Dunn components address how some learn best while being in a quiet environment while others prefer sound surrounding them. Or, some people wait till the last minute to do work while others begin immediately and complete projects before moving on to another one. Then again, some prefer to work alone while others prefer a partner or two. Of course, there's also one's pace and ability level, as well as learners' needs. All of these components constitute differentiating instruction. So, you may think, we all learn differently and sometimes there may be similarities, but the bottom line is: "We all have different abilities, and special needs that require different ways of providing instruction, because overall, we remember that which made a significant impact on our lives. That imperative is evident when we realize that we may not be the same, but we can learn the same material that's part of the curriculum (Schiering, 2014–present) depending on how it's presented.

Concerning instruction, a possibly little-known fact is that in the 1930s, varied types of learning with respect to what made an impression on individuals' retention was referred to as *experiential learning*. John Dewey was given credit for this idea, which was innovative in its time. Simply stated, individuals learned from their experiences. In the early 1990s the name was changed to *constructivism*, but both concepts remain the same in their basic premise is that each individual constructs meaning from his or her own experiences, and it is that experience that makes an impression and has now come to be considered at the core of teaching and learning strategies.

The IM addressed, along with its components, in this book may be explained with the following scenario:

> Think about making a footprint in the snow or sand. How was that impression made? In your mind's eye you can see it and envision how deep, how wide, and how long it is. Each aspect depends on the one making that mark in that place. So it is with teaching by using differentiated instruction. Each person is different, and each needs or requires instruction that will make an impression that lasts. However, the significance of how it was made will last longer than the actual footprint, because of the persons involved, the place it occurred, and the way it was done: Special needs, different abilities, and different ways!

In a discussion with Rickey Moroney, a colleague at Molloy College, Rickey mentioned the possibility of another factor regarding instruction being differenced for student learners, noting that "there's the importance of how a learner *receives* and *interprets* the subject matter presented." Hence, the *social cognition* component mentioned in the first paragraph of this preface is addressed. This social cognition is referred to and experienced all the time in the classroom; it is naturally present through the conversations we have with one another.

So while the method of instruction is very important as the focal point of this book, with examples for meeting the needs of student learners, so too is the concept that we are always learning. And "[w]e are all teachers of something" (Schiering, 2000–present; 2018). That "something" is what we model through our character and examples of learning techniques to help varied learners achieve success in the classroom setting. That last component leads to success and self-confidence in one's own interactions with others, both inside and outside of school.

Special Needs, Different Abilities and its companion book are based on concepts realized by my decades of experience teaching with the IM, yielding the best results regarding student academic and social success. "Direct experience through play on a particular topic not only enhances memory and the cognitive functions associated with memory, but also can be considered empowering. And, this happens independently of the condition of the learner, whether they are impaired or not impaired, from one country to another" (Schiering, 2015, p. 152).

Prelude

Question: Why use different ways to instruct children with special needs and/or different abilities?

Answer: The basic reasons for using differentiation of instruction and specifically, the Interactive Method (IM)/learning through active engagement/experientialism are to:

1. have different ways of instruction on which one can rely for the purpose of recalling material;
2. realize that whatever way one learns is acceptable, and learning through "doing" or being involved in the instructional method has been proven to provide "maximum retention of information" (Maheshwari, addressing Dale's *Cone of Experience*, 2016);
3. prepare the individual to do well on tests or exams;
4. have means that can be continually utilized for creating memories, at home if not in the school;
5. offer an entry-level means of instruction for developing a sense of self-confidence, efficacy, and reliance as well as skills necessary to face future learning challenges;
6. transition from the "different ways" by embracing one's own ability to learn when it is job time as opposed to schooling time; and
7. have means to rely on, at any stage of one's life, learning with comfort.

Question: Who benefits from the Interactive Method?

Answer: All types of learners benefit from the IM, because all learners are personally involved in their own learning. All types of learners includes English language learners (ELL) as well as those with attention deficit disorder and those others listed in chapter 1 under the heading "Types of Disabilities and Characteristics."

Acknowledgments

This book and its companion are about special needs, different abilities, and different ways to teach as well as learn. For the last of these, I have realized that no book is written without the assistance from a multitude of people. The ones at home probably come first. After that there are those who contributed through their writing, those who provided encouragement, and those who are in both of those categories.

There's not just assistance given for this book, but ones that came before it—and if I mentioned all those people, this section would possibly be longer than this book itself. The reason for this is that one event leads to another, perhaps not right away, but at some point there is a connection. There's a bringing together of the people in our lives who were part of events to which there was a reaction, which led to another event, and another reaction . . . until the book gets written. At this juncture, I thank the following:

I give sincere appreciation to my husband, George. He literally devoted himself to keeping me on task and did myriad other things. Some of these include: photos and figures for this book and the companion book (nearly one hundred in all), making photocopies of needed material, conducting research pertinent to the topic of both books, sharing with me what was most effective about my conference presentations, as well as proofreading the drafts of both books. As if this were not enough, he created the website www.creativecognition4U.com, which features videos he recorded about how to make the interactive instructional resources as well as lesson photographs of teachers using different ways with the Interactive Method. He also worked as a research assistant on this book and others I've written.

A few sentences before this one, I mentioned how one event leads to another. Such is the case with the chairman of the Royal English Department (RED) at Molloy College, Robert Kinpoitner, PhD. Bob is acknowledged for his helpfulness, for being a person who gives without asking for anything in return. I thank him for arranging for me to teach a children's literature course for the RED, and also for being my grammarian on all of the books I've authored. He is additionally recognized for his impeccable sense of humor and for continually being a person who lifts one's spirits with his positivity.

I must recognize Angela Sullivan, a contributor to chapter 2 of this book, for being present! Her organizational skills provided assistance, but most importantly, her friendship has been steadfast since we wrote together during our doctoral candidate years, twenty years ago. Once a teacher, then a school administrator and presently a professor, she continually practices and supports the ideas of the Interactive Method.

I thank Drew Bogner, PhD, president of Molloy College, for his coauthorship of *Teaching and Learning: A Model for Academic and Social Cognition* and most significantly for providing techniques addressing the "voice" of a book. His encouragement in the early 2000s served as the push I needed to start my writing endeavors at our institution.

Those who contributed to this book must be given acknowledgement of the highest degree for taking time to write and share their expertise with respect to teaching and/or life experiences with special needs or different abilities persons. Contributors include, Drs. Madeline Craig and Trish Eckardt, who wrote the foreword for this book; Drs. Angela Sullivan, Robert Kinpoitner, Pat Mason; Professors Rickey Moroney, Maggie Blair, Marie Calder, and Tim Ryley; Kevin Cooney, who is the Kiwanis Club adviser to Molloy's Circle K; Marc Hoberman; Clare King, a former teacher candidate and current special education technology teacher; Diana Abourafeh from the Rebecca Center for Music Therapy at Molloy; and Matthew and Jolie Schiering, two of our six children, who wrote for this book about the effect of interactive instructional techniques on leadership building and thoughts on being a resource room special education teacher, respectively.

I acknowledge Eileen Chapman with gratitude for transcribing figures into PDFs and for her formatting endeavors for this first book as well as portions of the companion one. Eileen also did this work for the book *What's Right with You: An Interactive Character Development Guide*. Eileen is a former colleague who became a friend and has been steadfast in assisting me with the technological components of writing.

This book has two contributions from teacher candidates. However, the companion to this book, *Achieving Differentiated Learning: Using the Interactive Method Workbook*, has contributions from more than one hundred of Molloy's former or present teacher candidates. They are acknowledged here because of the work they have done to support and infuse interactive learning. These individuals took the time to use IM in their classrooms or during student teaching, applying instructional techniques that used activity-based learning and/or Project/Performance-Based Learning (P/PBL) to pass along to others who teach special needs and different abilities students.

Tom Koerner, PhD, is a person whom happenstance presented to me. His publishing acumen, insight, and encouragement are unequaled. After seeing a few Interactive Book Report samples, he encouraged me to write about this activity-based strategy. This resulted in the publication in 2016 of *Teaching Creative and Critical Thinking: An Interactive Workbook*, as well as books before and after that, including one on character development. He has been most instrumental in all of my publishing endeavors, offering advice and support. His associate Carlie Wall has also been helpful with furthering my writing endeavors with her guidance and interest.

There are others along the path of having one's book(s) published whose work is of utmost importance. These are the production editors and copyeditors. These individuals cross check what needs to be addressed in the manuscripts for clarification of thoughts or references and a myriad of other things. This occurs before the manuscript goes to typesetting. Respectively for the first and second books there are production editors Megan DeLancey and Lara Hahn and copyeditors Meghann French and Julia Loy who I thank for being mindful.

Again, as one thing is connected to another I must acknowledge my tenth-grade social studies teacher, Ms. Carragher, who said, "I believe in you." These four words led me to think that if she could do that then perhaps I might believe in myself as well. And, as one's experimental past affects the present and future, the following are acknowledged for the idea of assisting others along life's paths: my parents, Mollie and Red After; my friend Daisy Schneider; and Rita Dunn, who served as my mentor in the St. John's University Instructional Leadership Doctoral Program. Her guidance brought me to presenting at schools here and abroad, as well as writing chapters in books. Her encouragement lives on with me to this day.

Last but not least are our children and their significant others: Matthew and Maddy, Alyssha and Paul Miro, Josh and Katie, Jolie, Mara and Dave Moore, and Seth and Carolina. And of course, our grandchildren—Jared, Rayna, Jacob, Bailey, Marina, Landyn, Eva, Eliana, Sam, Jonas, Levi, and Jewel—are appreciated for keeping me involved in what's "in" right now.

Introduction

This book defines the terms *special needs* and *different abilities* while providing a few strategies for activity-based instruction that address "different ways" to teach and learn. In that vein, the book focuses on the concept of *not* teaching the same thing the same way to student learners, regardless of grade level, at the same time. Instead, this book emphasizes the idea of distinguishing instruction to meet the necessities of all learners. As Dr. Rita Dunn stated, as far back as the 1970s, and specifically in 1996, "If children don't learn the way we teach, then we must teach them the way they learn."

That's well and good, you'd most likely agree. However, there first seems to be a call for clarification that the term *special needs* is not only about students with disabilities, but describes those who are *gifted*, or excel beyond their peers in the academic arena. There are also those students who, while doing well academically, are considered *disabled* because of emotional or behavioral factors, or those who are *twice exceptional*, or 2E, demonstrating giftedness in some subject areas and disabilities in other ones. "Additionally, there are those who are culturally and/or linguistically diverse and fall into this category" (Blair, 2018). Thus, it's comprehensible that the idea of special needs covers a wide range of individuals' academic aptitude.

Chapter 2 addresses present day 1) Response to Intervention and 2) Individual Education Programs (IEP). Each of these discusses what you may do to help different abilities learners. Then, in this second chapter there's examining how you process information. Hmm, that requires a good deal of thinking. This thinking, when verbalized, is part of classroom socialization and as such is addressed in the following chapter's IM section, regarding engaging students in learning and how this provides self-efficacy.

In chapter 5, why we remember some things and don't recall other things is discussed, and the three types of memory are defined. In this chapter you are also asked to use reflection and call to mind, for sharing, a pleasant recollection. In chapter 6 we turn to the many plusses of the IM, how it can be used as an alternative means of assessment, and how being involved in one's learning is part of leadership building.

The last three chapters of part 1 provide an introduction of the Reciprocity of Thinking, in chart format; the Cognitive Collective, which is a combination of thinking and feeling and how to distinguish one from the other; and definitions and examples of each thinking skill in the three phases of Beginning Awareness, Critical and Creative Thinking, and Metacognitive Processes, noting that there is movement within and between each phase from prelanguage on to late adulthood.

The second part of this book provides an overview of the Different Ways concept of teaching and learning, which is discussed in detail in the companion book. Part 2 also includes personal narratives that address disabilities and diversity, autism awareness, engaging those with exceptionalities, and personal experiences with epilepsy, all written from the contributors' personal experiences. The final chapter closes with the authors summative comments. Each chapter features a series of questions to address in journal or discussion format, with the latter preferred for social literacy in sharing of thoughts, ideas, opinions, judgements, and/or feelings.

BOOK'S AUDIENCE

This book is for you! Who "you" are is a learner and teacher, as these titles are used interchangeably. As one learns, one teaches, and vice versa. This book is for those who want to engage student learners in viable instructional situations that are enjoyable, because of their personal involvement. It's for those who love to discover, through instructional techniques, the finding of wonderment in learning by using different means of instruction that are suited to interests of their own or student-learners securities, methods, pace, ability level, perceptual preferences, processing styles, creative elements, and/or use varied types of instructional assignments for students achievement at the highest levels. This book is also for appreciating you, finding self-acceptance and inspiration in the way you teach!

Author's Philosophy

- As each of us is an individual, we each have special needs that require differentiation of instruction.
- What we think and feel becomes what we say and do.
- Memory is formed from one's emotional involvement in experiences.
- We learn and teach simultaneously, and we're all teachers of something.

- Project- and performance-based learning situations allow for personal involvement and retention of material.
- In order for effective learning, the educational setting must be a comfort zone for this shared environment.
- Conversation with others, self-appreciation, and instructional opportunities that involve the learner in self-efficacy provide viable opportunities for success, personal and academic.
- One classroom rule: No put-downs . . . only lift-ups!
- Through assignments that promote personal involvement, self-acceptance follows with the ingrained concept, "I am enough."

Part I

Information Gathering and Distribution Concerning Special Needs and Different Ability Learners

Chapter One

Reaching/Teaching Varied Learners

This chapter speaks to the relationship between "different abilities" and "special needs" in order to gain insight about these two student learner categories. These types of groupings are part of the heterogeneous classroom. *Reaching and teaching* all students are the operative for one's comprehension of the classroom's students. Basically, in order to teach the student you need to reach that student. This chapter and the rest of this book, as well its companion, address varied ways to influence learning and implement strategies that have proven to be successful for those with different abilities and special needs.

Behavioral characteristics of special needs persons are presented with definitions of *learning disabilities* as well as *types* of these to aid in recognizing the wide range of classifications regarding *different abilities*.

When a label or classification is attached to a particular student, what happens is the ability of that individual is not necessarily questioned. That aptitude level has already been determined. Even if a student is labeled a high achiever, the labeling or classification may work against that individual's living up to or falling short of the moniker.

Subsequently, this author suggests that labeling of student learners is not beneficial for the learner. Instead of this labeling or classifying, it is suggested a focusing on students' strengths should occur. So, take the emphasis off labeling and put it on thinking about what one "can or may do." Such thinking is productive and demonstrates positivity.

EXPLAINING ABILITIES AND NEEDS: REACHING AND TEACHING

Is there a difference between *abilities* and *needs*? While the former indicates one's capabilities, the latter refers to one's necessities, lack of aptitude, or disability. In any heterogeneous classroom there is a mixture of these types of student learners. Commonly, you have those who work above, at, and below grade level, as well as those who require more instruction due to learning insufficiencies. This last type of learner is considered *at risk*.

Overall, instructional methods that work for one group or individual may not work for another. That may seem as obvious as the idea that we need to reach students before we can teach them; if it is not, the following pages of this chapter and those in the accompanying book provide methods and techniques that engage student learners. This is accomplished by first comprehending their situation and then trying different ways to guide and/or instruct them.

As mentioned in the introduction, special needs students are often regarded as those with learning disabilities or difficulties, but it should be noted that those who are considered gifted also fall into this category. How do you suppose those ability differences are determined? It could be by variance in test scores, a physical abnormality, doing well on some assessments or task, but not on others, so that an inconsistency is observable. Overall, within each of these aforementioned groups there are varied levels of aptitudes. While some learners work above grade level in some subject areas, they may be at grade level in others. Some students are gifted and have special needs or disabilities in varied subject areas simultaneously.

Subsequently, different abilities are part of each classroom, and each of us has special needs of one sort or another, whether academic, social, physical, or emotional. *In order to teach our students, we first need to reach them.* Understanding what constitutes different ways of instruction first begins with knowledge of this portion of the book's title: "Special Needs, Different Abilities." In order to reach students, we need to know each one academically and understand their emotional perspectives/social cognition attitudes regarding learning and the classroom in general.

Question: So how do we teach these students?

Answer: We teach them the way they best learn. And, in my opinion, "we use differentiated, interactive instruction for memory acquisition and retention" (Schiering, 1984).

DEFINING LEARNING DISABILITIES AND TYPES OF DISABILITIES

Definition

As early as 1968 the U.S. Office of Education defined Learning disability as "a disorder in one or more of the basic psychological processes involved in understanding or in using language, spoken or written, which may manifest itself in an imperfect ability to listen, speak, read, write, spell, or to do mathematical calculations."

Subsequently, synthesizing material read on this topic over the past few decades, this author defines learning disabilities as involving students who may not see letters the way others do, they may not be able to pick out important features in a picture at which they're looking, and they may take longer to process a question or comment directed to them. They may also have difficulty following directions, attending to tasks, organizing their assignments, and managing time. Sometimes, these students appear to be unmotivated or lazy.

The following definitions of types of learning disabilities are unpublished, but compiled (2008) from various sources by Dr. Angela Sullivan during her assistant principalship at Thiells Elementary School.

Types of Disabilities and Characteristics

- Some causes of *speech and language disorders* include hearing loss, neurological disorders, brain injury, intellectual disabilities, drug abuse, physical impairments such as cleft lip or palate, and vocal abuse or misuse.
- *Dyslexia* is a general term for disorders that involve difficulty in learning to read or interpret words, letters, and other symbols, but that do not affect general intelligence.
- *Dysgraphia* is a deficiency in the ability to write (primarily handwriting) but also a difference in coherence. Dysgraphia is a transcription disability, meaning that it is a writing disorder associated with impaired handwriting, orthographic coding (orthography, the storing process of written words and processing the letters in those words), and finger sequencing (the movement of muscles required to write).
- *Mental retardation* is a genetic disorder that manifests in significantly below average overall intellectual functioning and deficits in adaptive behavior. Mental retardation is a particular state of functioning that begins in childhood and is characterized by decreased intelligence and adaptive skills.

- *Emotional disturbance* refers to any mental disorder not caused by detectable organic abnormalities of the brain and in which a major disturbance of emotions is predominant: affective disorder, emotional disorder, major affective disorder, mental disorder, and mental disturbance.
- *Attention deficit disorder* is a biologically based condition causing a persistent pattern of difficulties resulting in one or more of the following behaviors: inattention, possible hyperactivity, impulsive actions, and difficulty attending or focusing on a specific task.
- *Attention deficit hyperactivity disorder (ADHD)* is a brain disorder marked by an ongoing pattern of inattention and exhibition of hyperactivity-impulsivity that interferes with functioning or development, as well as one's performance.
- *Twice exceptional (2E) learners* "have the characteristics of gifted students with the potential for high achievement and give evidence of one or more disabilities as defined by federal or state eligibility criteria." Because of these learning and attention issues, 2Es "often find difficulty in the school environment, where organization, participation, and long-term planning play a role." (NAGC, n.d.)
- *Autism* (also called *autistic disorder*) is a variable developmental disorder that appears by age three and is characterized by impairment of the ability to form normal social relationships, by diminishing of the ability to communicate with others, and by repetitive behavior patterns.
- *Asperger syndrome* (also known as *Asperger disorder*), is an autism spectrum disorder that is characterized by significant difficulties in social interaction and nonverbal communication. These appear alongside restricted and repetitive patterns of behavior and interests, unusual or unusually rigid behaviors and interests, and unusual responses to stimulation and environment.
- *Hearing impairment* refers to a hearing loss that involves a partial or total inability to hear. A deaf person has little to no hearing. Hearing loss may occur in one or both ears. In children, hearing problems can affect the ability to learn spoken language; in adults it can cause work-related difficulties.
- *Visual impairment* refers to any visual condition that impacts an individual's ability to complete successfully the activities of everyday life. Students with visual impairments include infants, toddlers, children, and youth who experience impairments of the visual system that impact their ability to learn.
- *Deaf-blindness* is a term commonly used to describe individuals with a combination of impaired vision and hearing. *Dual sensory loss* and *dual sensory impairment* are other terms used to describe deaf-blindness.
- *Orthopedic impairment* may be caused by congenital anomalies, such as absence of a member or clubfoot; by disease, such as bone tuberculosis or

poliomyelitis; or by other causes, including amputations, fractures, cerebral palsy, burns, or fractures.
- *Traumatic brain injury* refers to damage to brain tissue caused by an external force and at least one of the following: a documented loss of consciousness, an inability to recall the actual traumatic event (amnesia), skull fracture, posttraumatic seizure, or brain scan abnormality because of the trauma.
- *Other health impairment* is a term that encompasses issues such as limited strength, vitality, or alertness, including a heightened alertness to environmental stimuli that results in limited alertness with respect to the educational environment. These impairments may be the result of chronic or acute health problems (including asthma, attention deficit disorder or attention deficit hyperactivity disorder, diabetes, epilepsy, a heart condition, hemophilia, lead poisoning, leukemia, nephritis, rheumatic fever, sickle cell anemia, or Tourette syndrome) and adversely affects a child's educational performance.

With these sixteen types of disabilities or different abilities defined, we can turn to questions regarding how best to teach these students and how teachers and/or students envision instruction techniques.

AN IDEA ABOUT *DIFFERENT ABILITIES* AND *SPECIAL NEEDS*

It seems that, as a society, we readily accept that children have *different abilities* in the academic arena. However, the term *special needs* carries a negative connotation, as it often refers to those who are at risk of failing in a particular subject area or grade. Individuals with the various disabilities listed in the previous section are characterized as having a "learning problem."

But what if we stopped pigeonholing these learners into categories that emphasize what's wrong and instead focused on their strengths? Or what if we, as educators, started saying what these learners *can* do, as opposed to what they *can't* do? Perhaps we could find alternative means of instruction or differentiated instruction to assist them in their learning endeavors. (There are a multitude of these in the companion to this book.)

A student who excels or works above grade level is also one who falls under the umbrella of special needs. In a manner of speaking, this giftedness is simultaneously an advantage and a disability, and these learners have special needs *because* they excel in learning. There's also the twice exceptional student who excels in some areas and does poorly in other ones because of a disability. Comparisons among learners are made in the classroom by teachers and students alike; it is important to instead focus on addressing students' strengths, as opposed to their learning difficulties.

FROM NEGATIVE TO POSITIVE

A shift from the negative to the positive in thinking regarding teaching special needs and different abilities student learners may be accomplished, in part, by schools' use of the three-tier Response to Intervention (RTI) program alongside an Individualized Education Program (IEP) to address each student's specific learning needs. This is explained in detail in the next chapter, and the companion book provides concrete examples of activities for the classroom in which different ways of instruction may be implemented.

In the next chapter Dr. Angela Sullivan, a retired school administrator and presently an adjunct professor, explains the use of the RTI program for different abilities and special needs/at-risk students. She addresses how the first two tiers of RTI are designed and how they assist, through different ways, students with varied abilities. She then references the third tier and explains the IEP. Following the RTI and IEP, Sullivan uses ideas from Tomlinson (1995) regarding suggestions for a differentiated classroom and also addresses classroom organization.

JOURNAL AND/OR DISCUSSION QUESTIONS

1. What is one difference between special needs and different abilities students?
2. What are five behavioral characteristics of special needs students? Explain each one.
3. What are three types of learning disabilities and how would you describe each one?
4. What was the "idea" presented in this chapter about different abilities and special needs?
5. What was the essence of the final section "From Negative to Positive"?

Chapter Two

Response to Intervention, Individualized Education Program, Classroom Organization

RTI AND IEP: AN EXPLANATORY NARRATIVE, ANGELA SULLIVAN, EDD

In today's educational environment, all students are expected to receive the same level of instruction from schools, and all students must meet the same set of standards. Expectations for students with learning disabilities are the same as students without any learning issues. It is now unacceptable for schools or teachers to anticipate less from one segment of students because they have physical disabilities or learning incapacities. As a classroom teacher, this mind-set of student achievement success cannot be attained without a true understanding of differentiation of instruction and special education. The mind-set must be that all students can achieve.

Differentiated instruction and special education share a singular goal, and that is to modify instruction until it meets the needs of all learners. As the student population has grown increasingly diverse in readiness levels and learning profiles, teachers recognized that they can't reach all students with a one-size-fits-all approach to instruction. Differentiated instruction emerged as a fully developed model in 1995 (Tomlinson) and has grown exponentially ever since. The goal of a differentiated classroom is "to maximize student growth and individual success" (Tomlinson & Allan, 2000, p. 4) by providing many avenues for students to acquire content, to process information and ideas, and to develop products.

"Emerging research demonstrates that differentiated instruction, when fully implemented, can significantly improve student achievement" (Goddard, Goddard, & Tschannen-Moran, 2007). Response to Intervention was originally conceived as an excellent way to instruct students with learning problems. Unlike the traditional discrepancy formula, which waited for students to fall far behind in his or her work, RTI identifies struggling students early on and provides increasingly intensive levels (or tiers) of support depending on how students respond (National Center on Response to Intervention, n.d.). A method of differentiating instruction found to be successful is to use interactive instructional resources.

No widely accepted definition of RTI exists, and adding to the confusion many teachers and principals experience, attempts at definition commonly focus on students at risk of academic failure. For example, the RTI Action Network defines RTI as a multi-tier approach to help struggling learners. Students' progress is closely monitored at each stage of intervention to determine the need for further research-based instruction and/or intervention in general education, in special education/resource room classes, or both.

Because of their differing origins, differentiated instruction and RTI are usually seen as separate initiatives. Both approaches are flexible in their implementation and may appear quite different from school to school or even from teacher to teacher, but both are built on two basic concepts: (1) Education is most effective when we treat students as individuals with different levels of readiness, learning profiles, and interests; and (2) teachers have a professional obligation to help all students succeed.

Tier 1 of RTI consists of regular classroom instruction provided to all students. *Within-classroom differentiation*, such as flexible grouping and individualized supports, should be a routine part of such instruction. Some of the time the teacher may be delivering whole-class instruction; at other times, students will be working individually or in flexibly grouped teams toward a common learning goal. The teams may be composed of learners with similar readiness levels (as determined by a combination of ability and achievement levels), interests, or learning styles.

If students are grouped by readiness level, some groups may have more structure in their work or more time to complete their assignment; others may have more complex problems to address. If the students are grouped by interests or preferences, some student groups may be writing, some acting out concepts, some designing a computer presentation, and some working on an oral presentation.

In other words, a classroom implementing RTI will first and foremost look like a differentiated instruction classroom. The major component that makes it not *just* a differentiated classroom but also an RTI classroom is that, in addition to typical classroom assessment (both formative and summative), the teacher keeps detailed records to monitor the progress of students who are struggling and who may need more intensive Tier 2 support. This intense monitoring and documentation facilitates differentiation as well, because it enables teachers to keep a continuous finger on the pulse of student progress and thus design differentiated lessons most accurately.

Students who do not make adequate progress in Tier 1 may be placed in Tier 2, which means that they receive interventions designed to address their areas of difficulty. These interventions address specific student's needs and form an Individualized Educational Plan (IEP). Such a plan may include *structural differentiation*—providing resources beyond the immediate classroom, such as reading specialists, cluster groups, or gifted education services. Again, the major difference between structural differentiation and services provided in Tier 2 is that Tier 2 requires more extensive documentation and perhaps more frequent assessment than Tier 1, giving attention to their special needs.

Tier 3 is a more specialized level of service that goes beyond what we usually regard as differentiation—for example, students' schedules may include significant amounts of time receiving intensive instruction in special education or talented classes or alternative schools. But the philosophy remains the same: regarding each student as an individual, asking what each student needs to be successful, and then using whatever services or structures are needed to support that success. Subsequently, while one refers to "differentiation," it should be emphasized that this includes, at its core, student engagement in the learning process . . . hands-on work.

SUGGESTIONS FOR CLASSROOM ORGANIZATION

As Angela Sullivan explains, many teachers fear or have a sense of concern that they do not know exactly what will happen when students experience a variety of classroom tasks and when teachers use different ways to instruct that student population. She relates that it is necessary that the teacher should have keen awareness of what and how students are doing. Therefore, it is recommended that teachers consistently review students' progress in using different types of lessons. Here are some helpful ideas from Sullivan's research about ways to stay organized and aware of how a classroom's organization is helpful for teachers and their students.

- Use student work folders. These always stay in the classroom and contain all work in progress (including partially completed tasks, independent study work, and anchor options). The folders also should contain a record-keeping sheet. Students document work they have completed and date of completion. Students also should note individual conferences they've had with the teacher, reflecting conversations about progress and goals. These folders provide an effective way to review student progress and may be

useful for parent-teacher conferences and conferences among parents, teachers, and students.
- Make a list of all skills and competencies you want your students to master in each facet of each subject (for example, in writing, spelling, reading, and grammar). Turn the skills into a checklist. Sequentially arrange the competencies on the left and put spaces for several dates and comments across the rest of the page beside each competency.

  Make one checklist for each student and keep the lists alphabetically in a notebook. Periodically spot-check students' work using the checklist, or do a formal written or oral assessment with individuals or the group from time to time. As you record observations over time, you should see a clear pattern of individual growth. This method will help monitor student progress; it also should help in developing differentiated assignments targeted to student need. These observations may aid in student-teacher planning conferences.
- Establish carefully organized and coded places where students should place completed assignments (for example, stack trays, boxes, or folders). This is much more effective than having assignments brought to you, and it is more effective than having a variety of assignments not organized.
- Carry a clipboard around the class with you much of the time. Make brief notes about things you see students do. Use the notes for reflection, planning, and individual and classroom conversations.
- Help your students see how important it is to complete activities so they become more and more skilled and insightful. Use peer checkers when an accuracy check is necessary. When it's time for formal assessment, help students see the link between good practice and success.

JOURNAL AND/OR DISCUSSION QUESTIONS

1. What is the definition of Response to Intervention?
2. How would you explain the purpose of an Individualized Education Program?
3. What are two ways explained in this chapter that address classroom organization? Qualify your answers.

Chapter Three

Individual Processing Style and Social Cognition

The first part of this chapter addresses individual processing styles. This is followed by Diana Abourafeh's narrative about how one way of teaching doesn't meet the needs of all student learners in a classroom. Next, the chapter provides information regarding the impact of social cognition on the classroom atmosphere, where the feelings one has in a learning environment affect the learning that occurs, and also touches on the idea that each of us has special needs and different abilities.

This chapter also addresses classroom ownership and belonging, as well as the idea that through our behavior "we are all teachers of something and that is our character" (Schiering, 2018). Conversing with—as opposed to talking "at" or "to"—others is emphasized. The classroom as a comfort zone is also discussed in a section by Jolie Schiering.

PROCESSING STYLES

Keefe (1979) noted that the idea of *processing information* emerged from the reform movements of the 1960s and 1970s as a key element toward increasing instructional responsiveness to individual students' needs. Keefe and Languis (1983) describe this area of concentration as the consistent patterns of behavior and performance by which an individual approaches educational experiences: "Subsequently, the way one addresses information processing is the composite of characteristic cognitive, affective, and physiological behaviors. Combined, these serve as relatively stable indicators of how a learner learns, interacts with, and responds to the learning environment" (Schiering,

1999; Schiering and Dunn, 2001). Processing style or learning style preferences refer to neuropsychological and cognitive theories.

Taking a look at how individuals process information is only one way to address the different abilities and special needs of students. Referencing Dunn and Dunn as far back as the mid-1970s, these include, when studying new and/or difficult material: a desire for working alone or with others; preference for sound present or silence; a comfortable room design or a formal one; and bright lighting or soft illumination.

A portion of the way a person processes information relies on his/her intuitiveness. Taken from the Dunn and Dunn Learning Style Model (1976) the following learning style preferences include

- a particular room temperature,
- modality/perceptual preferences (auditory, visual, tactile, kinesthetic),
- structure or lack thereof,
- working on one project until it's done or working on several projects at the same time (and perhaps not finishing any or some of these),
- skipping snacks or lunch, or taking frequent breaks for food,
- partiality for sequencing material or seeing the whole picture,
- having a preferred time of day,
- mobility or lack thereof,
- working by oneself, in pairs, with peers, or on a team,
- having adult authority or varied groupings, and
- having a level of motivation, persistence, and sense of responsibility.

Basically, different instructional environments, resources, and approaches respond to different learning abilities and special needs through areas of *strengths* of the learner. This is not to say that addressing these processing style preferences will satisfy all the differences or needs of students, but rather that these should be taken into consideration when designing lessons, especially those that are interactive and involve collaboration or cooperation.

Ultimately, those who are physically comfortable in their learning environment are more likely to learn and to approach learning in a positive fashion than those who are continually working without recognition of their preferences. Consequently, differentiation of instruction is evidenced when learners of different abilities and special needs have their favored ways of learning acknowledged and addressed.

ONE WAY DOES NOT FIT ALL:
DIFFERENTIATED LEARNING, *DIANA ABOURAFEH*

As a music therapist, I have the pleasure of engaging in creative processes with individuals of all abilities. I engage my clients in interactive play through improvised music that is created spontaneously in the moment. Here-and-now music experiences seek to foster engagement, relatedness, and reciprocity (Bruscia, 1987; Nordoff & Robbins, 2007). Within the context of relationship through following a client's lead/interests, a music therapist can provide opportunities for growth in social and emotional capacities (Carpente, 2016). Can a music therapist also bring in pre-composed music? Absolutely! However, the most important part of the clinical work is being able to be flexible in the moment based on clients' needs. No individual is the same and so no music experience should sound the same. Therefore, one size does not fit all!

It is the height of the neurodiversity movement, in which the unique neurology and personhood of an individual, say, diagnosed with autism spectrum disorder, is considered a human diversity similar to ethnicity, nationality, gender, and socioeconomic status (Robertson, 2009). This idea challenges the stigmatization of disability and instead encourages healthcare professionals and educators to try to find ways to support and accommodate individuals of all abilities without disparaging the unique qualities of their neurological functioning (Jaarsma & Welin, 2012).

Finding ways to accommodate these individuals means professionals must acknowledge that people of all abilities have a blend of strengths and weaknesses in the areas of "language, communication, and social interaction, sensory processing and self-regulation, motor skill execution, goal-orientated and reflexive thinking, and planning" (Robertson, 2009, para. 5). Similarly, each individual's unique biology colors the way he or she sees the world. These individual differences may include differences in motor planning, auditory language processing, visual/spatial processing, or sensory modulation (Greenspan & Weider, 2009).

A combination of understanding each person's unique strengths, areas of needs, and individual differences aids in creating experientials that are catered to each person's needs and learning process. Ways of supporting and accommodating sensory needs, for instance, include using a yoga ball or trampoline for one who may need the vestibular or proprioceptive input. Of note, these tools may be used not for a sensory break, but during experientials, because this may be what the individual needs to be engaged in the moment. Surely this is dependent on the individual.

People have their own experiences and sensory profiles that affect how they take in the world around them. Music therapy experiences that cater to individual interests and individual differences have been shown to provide a sense of self-pride and self-fulfillment (Abourafeh, 2018b). Additionally, they have improved development in areas of social communication and building relationships (Carpente, 2016; Thompson & McFerran, 2015; Warren & Nugent, 2010; Sorel, 2004, 2010).

While these are achievements accomplished through therapeutic means, they demonstrate the importance of catering to individual differences and different learning styles. One music experience does not fit all, and it is up to service providers and educators to—yes—be prepared, but also be flexible enough to adapt in the moment to clients' individual needs so that they may be able to be successful and grow.

SOCIAL COGNITION: DIFFERENT ABILITIES AND SPECIAL NEEDS

Up to this point, the first part of this chapter has addressed the academic concept of different abilities and special needs. Focusing on each of these, this author thinks it important to discuss the classroom atmosphere for optimum learning. In so doing, the point-of-view that is expressed acknowledges every individual's having different abilities and special needs. These may involve academic situations, such as needing to have a test's questions read aloud to the student by the teacher instead of being read silently by the student. And then there are special needs involving common social norms, such as a preference to sit alone, as opposed to in a group, or something as simple as talking to think instead of thinking to talk about all sorts of topics.

Having taught special needs students for seven years early on in my career, I contend that each of us is special in some way. Each of us requires something out of the ordinary at some juncture. Social cognition involves the student in communicating with others in the class. Most commonly, this is about everyday things, such as favorite foods, where students are going (or have gone) on vacation, or favorite television programs, apps, or video games. Uncommonly, there is deeper communicating, such as sharing ideas and getting to know a person—beliefs and values, areas of interest, relationships or lack thereof, and thoughts on self, and sometimes significant incidents in the individual's life—on a deeper level. In order to reach a person to teach that person, it's important to see that person as an individual. I suggest having conversations *with* others to form a classroom community of learners and create a caring bond.

CLASSROOM ATMOSPHERE BEFORE ACADEMICS: CHARACTER

As related in this book's Preface, whether one's specialness is related to academic ability or emotional components, feelings, or attitudes, we are all special as much as "we are all teachers of something" (Schiering, 2000-present; 2018). How is that, you may question? It means that whether we have the college degree that certifies one as a teacher of a particular grade level or specified discipline, the title of "teacher" doesn't preclude our being a demonstrator of our "character" with one's demeanor. That is the "something" each of us teaches regardless of where one resides, works, travels or is being formally or informally educated, Our character is what is being taught, how we interact and treat others is observable by the way we act and conduct ourselves.

In a classroom, before the subject matter is taught, there needs to be an atmosphere that supports a comfortable learning environment. The reason for that is because this is a shared environment/space. It belongs to those occupying it. Subsequently, the character the teacher models sets the tone for learning to occur. A pleasant character equates with a place where learning may occur, formidably.

We teach first how to act and what's acceptable with regard to how others are treated and how one individual interacts with him/herself. This teaching is exhibited in the classroom or on the social plain. After traveling throughout this country and abroad, I noted character traits posted inside school buildings, on walls of a classroom, or in community centers. These traits included what I came to see as six internationally accepted traits of a person of good character. These are listed with explanations of each one as follows:

- *Caring:* demonstrating to oneself and others, in thoughts and actions, compassion, unselfishness, and interest through kind acts
- *Kind:* demonstrating to oneself and others, in thoughts and actions, caring in a concerned manner
- *Fair:* demonstrating to oneself and others, in thoughts and actions, listening to others; realizing that fairness means each person getting what he needs, but not everyone getting the same thing
- *Trustworthy:* demonstrating to oneself and others, in thoughts and actions, honesty, integrity, promise keeping, and loyalty
- *Respectful:* demonstrating to oneself and others, in thoughts and actions, courtesy, politeness, tolerance, open-mindedness, consideration, and appreciation
- *Responsible and exhibiting good citizenship:* demonstrating to oneself and others, in thoughts and actions, pursuit of excellence, accountability, self-control, thinking before speaking or acting, and reliability; within a community, practicing being courteous and acting in a civil and helpful manner are part of good citizenship

These characteristics exhibited in a classroom setting may serve to create a learning space and atmosphere of safety and well-being. This goes alongside talking with students about positivity. It is necessary, in my opinion, to provide opportunities to recognize students as individuals. It is also important to provide occasions for "sharing times" when these character traits are experienced or witnessed. An emphasis on conversation is essential; it is crucial to talk *with* students, as opposed just to giving directions or instructions and relating how things are to be done. This is vital for classroom ownership and sense of belonging.

The idea of students having different abilities and/or special needs is to acknowledge classroom students diversity, with embracing it, honoring everyone's uniqueness through acceptance of each other's learning preferences and strategies to which each responds most confidently. Certainly, before any subject matter is addressed, the idea of how to conduct oneself in the classroom and be considerate of others' "needs" is of upmost importance.

> Being a person of good character is a process that takes a lifetime to complete. These traits are learned responses that become natural through practice. (Schiering, 2000–present; 2017)

SPECIAL EDUCATION: A RESOURCE ROOM TEACHER'S VIEWS, *JOLIE SCHIERING*

I have thought long and hard as to what the definition of *special education* means to me as an educator, let alone what it means to my students. You have children who are aware they require services and those who are not aware and think time with a special education teacher is just "extra play time." You have parents, lawmakers, and administrators to consider what this definition really means in the teaching profession.

What does *regular education* even mean in today's world? We have grown beyond the days of past where special education was just a form of dyslexia, low IQ, or physical limitations. The field itself was not all encompassing in the past. Special education to an adult who is not special needs is very different from what special education is to the person who requires it or a parent who has to live with and adjust to life in the system itself.

I am a child of the "mild special education" population. Having to deal with dyslexia, speech impairment, and dysgraphia with the minimal support and knowledge about ways to help that were available back then, is mind boggling to me now that I was able to complete college and postgraduate work and become a published book contributor, all with assistance from my peers and educators who understood the basic concept of the meaning of *fairness*. Here I sit with the question: *What does special education mean to me?* In a recent visit to a spirituality connection class, I found my answer.

Special education is a means for those students who feel disconnected from others and from the educational process to feel, participate, and gain knowledge as a collective whole, helping to ignite a feeling of hope instead of rejection from the world at large. It is about relationship building and embracing your own uniqueness in the learning process. It allows one to feel a wholeness/togetherness in the learning process and build a true connection with an educator or fellow student, so as to not feel alienated by the rest of the world. Special education means taking a broken process cookie-cutter model and showing everyone it is okay not to fit the mold. That is my take on what special education means to me, and what I think it should mean to others.

Question: From your observations or experience, what are your viewpoints on the topic of special education being addressed in a resource room?

NEXT CHAPTER

The next chapter of this book addresses one's building toward the idea of differentiated instruction. This is accomplished with addressing students' diverse abilities and specialness using the concept of an Interactive Method (IM). Simplistically defined this method recommends using means of instruction involving creativity, imagination, and critical thinking while designing resources that are, ultimately, project and/or performance based, and involve differentiation of instruction while being self-corrective is recommended.

JOURNAL AND/OR DISCUSSION QUESTIONS

1. How would you explain, in detail, the term *processing style*?
2. What were three key points in the narrative titled "One Way Does Not Fit All: Differentiated Learning," by Diana Abourafeh?
3. In your opinion, what is meant by "classroom atmosphere before academics"?
4. What are the six international traits of good character, and what is one experience you've had with one of these or a time you witnessed that behavior? Please share this with another.

Chapter Four

The Interactive Method

Student Engagement and Self-Efficacy

In this chapter, differentiation and/or different ways of instruction are addressed through the Interactive Method (IM) of teaching and learning, including the IM components Interactive Book Report (IBR), Activity-Based Learning Centers (ABLC), and Project/Performance-Based Learning (P/PBL). Each of these learning/teaching strategies is explained and a bit of history is provided as well. Overall, each strategy engages students in experiential learning to increase their "remembering." The end result is a sense of self-efficacy and empowerment. This applies to all types of learners: those seen as a part of the mainstream as well as those with special needs and different abilities.

The eight components of an IBR are provided before the IBR's "effects" and "affects, as well as "attributes"; including "self-efficacy" of interactive learning. These components are analyzed for one's own opportunity to evaluate them. "The idea of using different ways to instruct is grounded in creating memories for the learner. Doing so calls for the retention of information for later use inside and outside the classroom. The method of instruction being that which utilizes perceptual preferences calls for mental and motor memory, which provides student empowerment and later may be applied for 'recall' when test taking occurs" (Schiering, 1996).

EXPLAINING THE IM AND DIFFERENTIATION OF INSTRUCTION

The concepts of differentiating instruction primarily referenced in this book are interactive learning that involves "educational gaming" and also involves instructional techniques that include either projects that result in performance or performances that lead to projects. All are addressed in the IM with the understanding that a *method* is a way of doing something. There's a set pattern but also a great deal of flexibility in that pattern, as will be seen later in this chapter in the section titled "Requirements of an IBR." Overall, the IM requires interaction, as opposed to implementing a Socratic method of instruction that involves students as the passive recipients of information.

Differentiation of instruction is the major component of the IM, and it is for all students, including those who have different abilities and require different ways of doing things, sometimes perhaps because of special needs. Most importantly, the IM covers a broad spectrum of instructional techniques. Its approach involves and engages students who are learning through inventing for the purpose of being creative, sharing ideas, and exchanging visions while being interactive, oftentimes through the development of interactive instructional resources.

Subsequently, the IM represents a means of learning and teaching that involves doing hands-on work, and also being creatively and imaginatively involved in the cognitive/thinking process, so much so that critical and creative thinking are at their zenith. The overall idea of these varied types of instruction or differentiation is that students partake in their own learning. A few examples appear in chapter 10 of this book, and the companion book features many activities based on the IM's differentiation of instruction, which involves, at its core, interactive learning.

The IM serves as a guide for performance tasks that include the inspiration for divergent (open-ended) thinking and use of imagination, promotion of independent learning, but involves design planning, with a finished product, and builds on prior experience or obtaining experience in general through construction of pages. This may be done through multimedia research.

Since many activities are done not by oneself, but rather in partnerships or small groups, these include classroom interaction and collaborative learning, self-assessment and self-reliance, as well as attention to identification and use of the skills on the Reciprocal Thinking Phases Chart (Schiering, 1999), which goes from comparing and contrasting to the metacognitive processes of recall and reflection.

The Three Major Activity-Based Components of the IM

1. An *Interactive Book Report* with educational games or interactive instructional resources in the five major disciplines of reading, English language arts (ELA), math, science, and social studies, as well as a creative game-type page. These are preceded by a title page; author review; story summary, which is a summary of the story or topic; Reciprocal Thinking Skills Identification Chart, a chart that names the activity and thinking skills used to play that page; and a welcome page or invitation to play the IBR pages. (Numerous examples of these playable pages appear in the companion book.)
2. *Activity-Based Learning Center*, which often involves simply taking pages from an IBR and enlarging them to poster size (or at least larger than notebook-sized paper), then placing them in an area of the classroom (using tri-fold boards or placed on tables) where one or more students may go when others are receiving more formal instruction. This area is referred to as an ABLC.
3. *Project/Performance-Based Learning* activities, which call for the creation of a product through the "project" portion, then addresses a showing of the product. This is similar to the IBR in that it involves the construction of something, but P/PBL might also entail research that is then presented in a performance-style display, rather than as a game-type activity. The interaction comes in the gathering of information and putting it together for a performance or sharing.

At its core a performance enables learners to demonstrate their knowledge aptitude by producing a project or product. These tasks allow for the use of real-life situations, rather than just providing information on a philosophy. With that in mind, there are many projects that may be done with a resultant performance.

Student Projects

These projects might include educational games; interactive instructional resources; graphic organizers involving decision making; varied types of books, drawings, and posters that advertise; bulletin boards; exhibitions; science experiments; computer, board, and wall games; acrostic or other types of poems; letters in a word family; foam-core board displays; brochures with instructions or information and illustrations; or dioramas, three-dimensional displays, and diagrams (Schiering, 1996).

Student Performances

These following examples are a few that would be considered a performance: poetry competitions; game shows; mock radio, television, or video broadcasts; mock television or radio broadcast; play or role-play; speeches; video clip interviews or informational pieces related to the topic such as weather; demonstration of a game made or something involving cooking or a craft project; debate; and/or storytelling (Schiering, 1996; 2015b; 2016; McTighe & Wiggins, 1999).

The IM's P/PBL Support Comment

When this author first heard about those student project-and-performance-based examples, what came to mind was learning that involved the experience of gathering information for later use in varied disciplines. Melissa Kelly, in an article for ThoughtCo.com, explains this method of interaction by stating, "[T]his is when students participate in performing tasks or activities that are meaningful and *engaging*. The purpose of this kind of learning is to help students acquire and apply knowledge, practice skills, and develop independent and collaborative habits" (Kelly, 2017).

Factoid

While there is a difference between presenting and performing, semantically, the idea of displaying an end product and sharing it with others joins the three types of the IM. Each one involves the student learners in designing and then creating a project in any discipline. The method of information gathering may be different, but the final component is the performance of presenting the product, which is what has been created, in a formal manner.

Clarifying the IM as a *Blanket*

You're asked to think about a cold winter's day. The outside temperature is hovering around zero degrees. Inside your home you are bundled up under a blanket, maybe watching television or seated at your computer. Wherever you are, that blanket is proving warmth, coziness, and security while keeping you comfortable. Think of the Interactive Method as being that blanket, as that's the best word to describe it. It covers or includes the IBR, ABLC, and P/PBL as instructional techniques that provide for the learner the same sense of comfort and security as the blanket used on a cold winter's day.

You may wonder why I refer to the IM as a *blanket* or *covering*. The answer is that this type of differentiation of instruction brings learning that is adaptable to students by addressing their use of imagination, creativity, design, construction, possibly research, and definitely critical thinking. Later, along with the student's sense of accomplishment, comes reflection with the use of memory to find success with mastery of any type of curriculum. This author thinks this is mainly because of the involvement/engagement/interaction of the learner in learning.

Important Notes

Another important facet to interaction with these components is that there is no age limit to learning through play or to the use of interactive instructional resources that one has made or that have been made by a classmate, friend, or parent. Also worth noting is that it is a well-researched fact that we remember that which has made an impression on us, and learning using an interactive means of instruction creates memories that are retained for future use both inside and outside the academic arena.

Interesting Fact

In 1998 the fifth-grade class I was teaching made a 3 1/2-foot-high and 20-foot-long *Interactive Earth Day Book*. This was a thematic unit of study and actually a very large IBR that became, because of its size, an ABLC. The individual panels were self-corrective educational games designed by the student learners. The panels were taped together and opened and closed accordion-style. Twenty-six students worked in partnerships to design at least one interactive instructional resource for each of 14-foam-core board panels.

For example, a Wraparound panel was designed and constructed as a matching game that involved weaving yarn from ecosystem-related words to their definitions. Vocabulary words used included *ecologist, succession stage, forest floor, water, land, living organisms, ecology,* and *biodegradable*.

When the panels were completed the students from other classes were invited to come in and play the panels. Next, pictures of it were taken and the classes' ABLC project was entered in the NYS *I'm a Green Nation Competition*. The actual ABLC was among six hundred entries and came in first place addressing the topic of reduce, reuse, and recycle. The Board was driven to Albany for a judging and then the actual day of awards the class, on a school bus, joined their work in Albany, NY. It was here that the governor of New York State awarded them a medal for their participation in this endeavor.

IBR, ABLC, AND P/PBL EVALUATION

The culminating presentation of the differentiation of instruction used in IM techniques most commonly results in some form of evaluation. While the activity—especially in the IBR or ABLC—is self-corrective, the presentation of these and the P/PBL may be formally assessed. This most likely is an observation; there may also be a rubric by which the end product in the performance or presentation part is addressed in a subjective manner.

Each of the IM's techniques involving differentiation of instruction is considered *authentic learning*, such as the creation of an interactive instructional resource or perhaps a newspaper/newsletter; videotaped broadcast of weather, news, events, or geographical areas of interest; or conducting a class debate where many viewpoints may be expressed nonjudgmentally.

The major benefit of these types of products in the IM's three components is the *active involvement* in the learning process, making it possible to absorb and understand the material at a deep level. The performance part requires presentation, which in turn develops speaking skills in front of an audience most simply through practice. This author notes that aside from using beginning and intermediary thinking skills, the IBR, ABLC, and P/PBL focus on deep/high-level thinking, as in the metacognitive processes discussed in chapters 7, 8, and 9.

Self-Correction

Since these interactive resources are self-corrective, the student develops, at the very least, *self-reliance* and *self-confidence* along with *self-efficacy*. Ultimately, no one learns the same way as another. We all have different abilities and some special needs, so varied interactive instructional resources provide the opportunity for learners to select their first, second, third, and so on way of learning.

Teacher Assessment Guides

Students should be aware of the requirements of the project and/or performance, with specific stated goals. The learning standards addressed in P/PBL should be available or the benchmarks noted, with the performance task or project as the culminating assessment. The use of the Reciprocal Thinking Phases Chart is important to help the student identify what skills are being addressed when "playing the pages" of an IBR or doing a project or performance. The grade is most likely to be nontraditional in that it may not be an actual letter grade but rather the level of achievement on each of the criteria.

Heidi Goodrich Andrade (2000) notes a few advantages of using rubrics as an assessment tool:

- Rubrics are used to improve and monitor pupils' performance by clarifying teacher expectations through rating the quality of the work.
- Rubrics guide self/peer assessment as they promote pupils' awareness of the criteria being used in assessing the work.
- Rubrics increase validly, reliability, and fairness in scoring. Provision for more objective and consistent assessment as criteria are clearly defined.
- Rubrics provide a profile of success and areas to be improved.

- Rubrics make learners aware of the learning objectives and hold them accountable.

Questions

What are some projects in which you've been involved or have a memory of because of your involvement in learning? What are some projects, activities, and performances you have in your classroom that involve your students, through interaction, learning a particular topic or subject area? Have you shared this technique of the IM or P/PBL with other educators, parents, and student learners? Why or why not?

A LITTLE IBR HISTORY

From the earliest training in the how-to of writing book reports, there were several pages of student written information addressing the six elements of a story: characters, setting, moods, events, problem and solution. These essay style accountings were about a storybook that was read, or topic to be studied. Topics usually addressed informational books or thematic units of study. For example, these book reports were on such topics as: pioneers, outer space, inventions, community helpers, USA Presidents, food chain, ecosystems, weather, Earth's solar system, butterflies, dinosaurs, or an historical event.

In the 1990s, after decades of reading students' book reports, as explained in the previous paragraph, this student writing and teacher reading process for review of a story, informational book or thematic unit of study became relatively boring. for this author. Each book report had nearly the exact same information and looked the same as well.

In 1996, after being in the Instructional Leadership Doctoral program at St. John's university, this author thought, "What about making an Interactive Book Report where each discipline is represented with an educational game?" Taking this idea, and making an outline of what would make-up an IBR, the student learners in the author's fifth-grade came to create the first IBR. In 2003 this author's ELA and reading teacher's candidates formed partnerships and made IBRs for elementary students on a piece of literature for grades 1–6.

No matter who is making the IBR, inventing pages to address the book or thematic unit is the operative! For an IBR on a piece of literature, one might create a matching page for characters and character traits (reading discipline), or a set of word opposite puzzle cards using words from the book's phrases and idiomatic expressions (task cards: ELA discipline).

For a thematic unit on butterflies, a science discipline page may be constructed for identifying the life-cycle of this animal. Making and displaying the final product addresses, for the page creator and then player, not just the aforementioned discipline but also ELA with sequencing. This is a critical thinking skill.

For any IBR types (piece of literature, informational book or thematic unit), the creator's imagination brings forth many ideas and involves application of thinking skills. And, for the activity user/page player, thinking skills are continually experienced. Most importantly, just providing the opportunity to be creative allows notions to flow and a multitude of thinking skills to be implemented and applied as learning operations.

Each IBR activity page entry addresses a particular subject area and is specifically designed to be educational game. And these pages are all to be self-corrective with respect to the disciplines of reading, English language arts, social studies, math, and science, as well as a "creative" page at the close of the IBR. If an automatic self-correction is not possible then put a sample of the way the page is to be done on the back of the activity for page-player reference.

The beauty of the IBR is that students may be inventive and creative while thinking critically to design pages related to specific disciplines as well as ones that attend to the six elements of a story. Many pages are playable and some are informational. The pages are created, for the most part, on plain notebook-sized paper and are collected in a two- to four-inch binder. The pages may be individually laminated or put inside a page protectors to keep them clean for multiple uses. Examples are provided in the companion to this book.

REQUIREMENTS OF AN IBR

1. *Title Page*: This page had the title of the storybook/piece of literature, informational book or thematic unit of study topic.
2. *Table of Contents*: This is a listing of the pages in the IBR in sequential order.
3. *Author Page*: The author page features information about the author. For example, *Cloudy with a Chance of Meatballs* by Ron Barrett might be used for a thematic unit on weather. For the IBR creator, the author page about Barrett would likely include internet research regarding his personal or literary life history. If the IBR is specifically on a unit of study, then an overview of the topic would be provided on this page.
4. *Book Summary*: The book summary page features a written narrative about the book that highlights the events of the story with respect to their scope and sequence. For a thematic unit of study, this page provides an overview of the topic; for example, in a thematic study of

weather this page might include information about and perhaps definitions of types of storms and various other weather conditions.
5. *Welcome Page/Invitation Page*: The welcome/invitation page is devoted to welcoming and inviting the reader to do the activities in the IBR. This is where the reader and page player of the IBR is asked to partake in the self-corrective activities to review the story or thematic unit of study. An example for an IBR on the topic of "weather" might be:

You're invited to play the pages of this IBR to learn about different types of weather. The subject areas of reading, math, science, English language arts, and social studies are playable pages, along with one I made up for you. Each page is designed to have you remember things about the topic of weather in an enjoyable way, by playing the pages of this IBR. Basically, the idea is to have fun learning. Turn the page and start enjoying learning by playing educational games.

Welcome Page/Invitation. You might try a bit of poetry:

> **Example of Welcome Page**
> Come play these pages and you will see
> How the "weather" impacts you and me.
> Each page is an educational game
> None are alike, none are the same
> You're invited to learn about "weather"
> So, play the pages and discover you're clever!

6. *Specific Discipline Pages*: There are five or more specific discipline pages in an IBR. The number of pages for each discipline (reading, ELA, science, math, social studies) is determined by the individual(s) making the IBR. One page per discipline is required. who decides how many pages will represent each discipline. If only one activity is designed for each discipline, then this portion of the IBR will have five pages. Each activity should be interactive and self-corrective.
7. *Creative Page*: This is a page the IBR creator makes-up by using his/her imagination. The page could be a role-play, instructions for a dance, or an acrostic poem. The important thing is that the creator of the page has designed an activity that's self- corrective or shows an example of what is expected as an end product for playing of the page or being physically involved in its being played. and is not necessarily any of the few activities in figures at the end this Book 1, nor the multitude of these activities in pictures with explanation for construction and usage in the companion book. It's something the IBR designer made-up on his or her own.
8. *Backs of Pages*: When opening the IBR the "facing page" is the one on the "right side" and the back of the page is what's behind it. For example, the title page would come first and the back of the front of

the binder would be on the left with the title page on the right side. Then, on the back of the title page is either blank or may have a quotation from the book, a picture that relates to the book, a positive encouraging statement (You're doing well? Keep up the good work?) or something that connects to the story, information topic, or thematic unit.

The facing page would be the table of contents on the "right" side. Then, on the back of that would be the same type of thing that's on the back of the title page. This occurs throughout the IBR unless there is a carry-over of a particular page and then it goes on the back and the "facing page" or one on the "right side" begins the new activity.

9. *Reciprocal Thinking Phases Identification Chart or Listing*: This page comes at the end of the IBR. You'll first need to look at figure 7.1 in chapter 7, as this is an overall view the Thinking Skill Phases and what skills are in each Phase. After this viewing and looking at each activity you have, decide which thinking skills are being used for that activity when you play that IBR page. Now, you may chart each activity by having four headings of: Activity, Phase One, Phase Two, and Phase Three. Then, under each Phase put the skills for each named activity. So, you'd have at least five horizontal columns.

Another way to do this is to make a paragraph for each activity. First, name the activity and then list, in Phase format, without columns, the skills you think are applied when playing the page. An example of this format would be:

Velcro Story Map: Phase One: Recognizing, Realizing, Identifying, Classifying. Phase Two: Prioritizing, Initial -deciding, Initial Problem-solving, Sequencing. Phase Three: Evaluating, Organizing, Advanced-deciding and problem-solving, reflecting, self-actuating.

See figure 7.1 in chapter 7, which provides a visual of this reciprocity of thinking in chart format. Also, in chapter 8 there is a listing of each thinking skill on the chart, and the definition of each skill, with an example of each one. Basically, the skills go from those involving Beginning Awareness (Phase 1) to Critical and Creative Thinking (Phase 2) and, lastly, Metacognitive Processes (Phase 3). This chart states the activity, discipline, and then has the thinking skills used for each activity page in the aforementioned subject areas with division of each by Phase (Schiering, 1999).

10. *Congratulations Page*: The last page of the IBR is one that "congratulates" the page reader and player. Since all pages are self-corrective for student empowerment and self-efficacy, there is no evaluation of the work done on the activity pages. The person does each activity page until mastered. No one needs to know, other than the student, if the activity or part of it needed to be repeated. This is a learning-

through-play project that has no evaluation other than one's own ability to do the activity. You may have an IBR maker signed certificate or simply the words "Congratulations on completing the IBR!"

POSSIBLE IM ACTIVITIES: IBR, ABLC, OR P/PBL

What follows is a list of activities that have been created by fifth-grade and/or college students for IBRs addressing either a piece of literature or a thematic unit of study. Directions for making the first five are located in the companion to this book, as well as in *Teaching Critical and Creative Thinking: An Interactive Workbook* (Schiering, 2016), as well as going to www.creativecognition4U.com.

- Flip-Chute
- Electro-Board
- Pic-A-Dot
- Task cards
- Wraparound
- Decision-making graphic organizer: This is an activity done on notebook paper or poster board. There is a stated problem in a textbox and under that are three choices to solve that problem. Under "Choice" are three Possible Positive Outcomes and three Possible Negative Outcomes. The textbox at the bottom of the page had the final decision on why this was made.
- Board game
- Velcro or magnet match
- Floor game: A shower curtain liner is needed to make this game. You use a permanent magic marker to have a flower drawing, for example. Then you have "question cards" that ask for the location of the different parts of the flower. On the back of the card put the drawing of the flower with an arrow to the flower part. The floor game person steps on the flower part named on the card and the person with the card checks to see if they're correct.
- Word search
- Who Said That?
- Cause and Effect graphic organizer
- Character chart
- Sequence of events
- Character trait match
- Map key
- Word opposites
- Venn diagram Hula Hoop Same and Different

- Periscope math: This is a two-person game. You'll need a cylindrical tube. In one end close to where you could look into the tube, put a slit that nearly goes through the tube. Do this again a few inches back from that slot. Make an index card with a math equation like "2+2" on the index card and put it into the front slot. Put the answer on a second index card in the second slot. When the person holding the tube answers the equation lift out the first card to reveal the answer on the second card. Make as many cards as you want with equations and answers.
- Deck of cards equations (equation on picture side of card and answer on flip side; for example, 7 + 3 = 10)
- Food chain stacking cups
- Three-dimensional crossword puzzle or word family identification chart with pictures (for example, *-at* family with members *cat, hat, bat, sat, fat, rat, mat, pat, vat*).

A LITTLE ABLC HISTORY

Over the past two decades, the use of in-class learning centers has come to the foreground as an instructional practice in elementary classrooms. This has accompanied or followed the concept of project and performance-based work, which Common Core Standards have emphasized over the past ten years. One idea that has come of this is not to use interactive instructional techniques for an IBR in only a binder or book format, as explained earlier, but rather to take one (or several) of these activities and place it on a poster board, a portion of a tri-fold board, or a table. This provides the opportunity for an Activity-Based Learning Center that places new educational games with ones already existing.

Beginning in the early to mid-1990s, the fifth-grade classes I taught included ABLCs based on interactive learning. These interactive tri-fold boards with their hands-on games were also given to elementary schools as learning centers. These are for a service-learning project of the freshman Children's Literature classes at Molloy College. These are done to demonstrate the advantages of interactive learning.

The center of a tri-fold board might feature a Story Map graphic organizer with the six elements of a story: characters, setting, moods, events, problem, and solution. The side flaps of the board might have three-to-a-side activities. These examples are found under "Possible IM Activities: IBR, ABLC, or P/PBL."

A specific example for a tri-fold board side flap would be a Task Card Holder filled with 20 task cards. These are 5x8 index cards that have a question on one side and an answer on the other side. Or there may be a picture on one side and identification or description of that picture on the other side. Yet another idea is a quote on one side and the name of the person who said it on the other side. Or, word opposites work well too.

These cards are then cut in half, but each one is cut in half differently. Let's say you were doing word opposites. On the left side of the card would be the word "TOP" and on the right side would be the word "BOTTOM." There could be an accompanying illustration of a building with an arrow directing one's view to the top of that structure and on the other side an arrow pointing to the lower portion of the building.

The task is to fit the cards together by matching the shapes. Put the cards on a desk top or floor and mix up these puzzle pieces for matching by the student learners. Clearly this is self-corrective as the student knows the opposite had been recognized by the matching of the cards.

DESIGN AND PURPOSE OF AN ABLC

To begin an ABLC, as mentioned in the previous section, the classroom students made activities (self-corrective educational games) for the side-sections of the Tri-fold Board. These could be on topics that address different disciplines. Examples would include Task Cards on adding, subtracting etc., or a Flip-Chute in ELA with vocabulary words and definitions, or science, depending on the Board's topic could have matching a picture of a climate zone with the word representing that area, and social studies and reading would also be educational games on the side pieces.

The making of what's on the Tri-fold Board would be done in partnerships or small group format, depending on class dynamics. A whole Board could be done by one student if that person so desired. To use these learning tools and educational games, I would designate, a forty-five-minute time slot as "Interactive Resources Exchange Time."

Basically, this was a dedicated time to share, with classmates, the different ABLC's. The idea was when reading the center section on, let's say, a piece of literature, there would be a basic understanding of the story without actually having read that story.

Or, if the ABLC was on a topic such as weather then the center section would have information on that to read. The side flaps would have, respectively, vocabulary from the storybook, perhaps comprehension questions or geography that related to the story.

For a unit on weather the side flaps might have Task Cards about weather or climate words, how to use math to tell when a storm is coming, have pictures of different climate zones and match them with their name. The basic purpose is that when the ABLC's are used by those not having made the Board, the material is learned in such a manner that students are teaching other students in the class through use of the ABLC, what interactive instructional resources the student learner or varied groupings had made.

The result of this reading and playing the educational games on the ABLC is that the students were empowered, learned from one another, had fun, were fully engaged, and appreciated their classmates' work as well as having a development of self-reliance.

Ultimately, no one learns the same way as another, so these IBR pages, converted into ABLCs or simply used as interactive instructional resources on different topics, provided opportunities for learners to select their first, second, third, and so on way of learning. Audios were made for auditory learners. PowerPoints were created and used by the most visual learners. Kinesthetic learners performed role-plays or played large board games, or floor games; coming up to the computer to use the SMART Board was also in the realm of whole-body involvement.

Several times learners designed three-dimensional word searches or crossword puzzles, created Jeopardy-style game, or used Kahoot on the computer on a specified topic, and/or math periscope or answer-equation match, to name a few games. Students determined their own learning process, selected the activities that worked best for themselves, and enjoyed this forty-five-minute "special" time of the day.

More Information: IM, IBR, ABLC, and P/PBL

The IM—with its IBR, ABLC, and P/PBL—may be used every day in the classroom, or wherever one is trying to learn new or formerly presented material. So the components of the IM may also be used once a week or a few times a month or once in a while, for most of a semester or throughout the year. Primarily, this decision depends on the individual using the methodology. The overall idea is that these activities address different ways of instruction for different abilities or special needs persons; they're different from traditional instruction.

Keep in mind that each of these interactive ways is always at the ready! And the method and resources address the idea that creative cognition is utilized along with critical thinking; they're intertwined, and are developed and enhanced by using the method or being involved in differentiation of instruction techniques. Additionally, these interactive pages involve learning and teaching being knotted, with the roles of the teacher being connected to those of the learners. As Delialioglu (2012) stated, "Students are more engaged when the instruction increases the contact between student and teacher, provides opportunities for students to work in cooperation, encourages students to use active learning strategies, provides timely feedback on students' academic progression, requires students to spend quality time on academic tasks, establishes high standards for acceptable academic work and addresses different learner needs in the teaching process."

Using self-corrective activities, instant feedback on the learner's academic acuity is clearly provided. Additionally, the active engagement of the learner's mind is predominant, as the inventiveness, creative thinking, and incorporation of imagination abound.

Reiteration

The IM—a blanket term that addresses interactive learning via the IBR, ABLC, and P/PBL—represents a means of learning and teaching that involves hands-on work and encourages creative and imaginative involvement in the cognitive/thinking process, so much so that critical and creative thinking are at their zenith.

EFFECTS AND AFFECTS: ADDRESSING DIFFERENT ABILITIES

Defining *Effect*

You've probably heard someone ask, "What effect did that have on you?" What this refers to is the end result, outcome, or conclusion of an incident or comment with respect to your perception of it. An example might be that I was not injured because I was watching where I was walking and avoiding tripping on the rock in the path. When someone commented on how lucky I was, I thought, "Yup, that's because I was focused on where I was walking."

In order for there to be an *effect* on a situation or someone, there needs to be an understanding of the means to realize a consequence or achievement, or to make something happen, as to bring it into being. Bringing the effect into realization with the IM, IBR, and ABLC may be (1) the *effect/result* of these caused learners to realize their critical thinking and creativity were part of their ability to imagine and invent; (2) the *effect* of their imagining and inventing resulted in bringing into being activities and learning through playing; (3) another *effect* was information retention; and (4) the *effect* of the method and strategy, together, made an impression on all who experienced it. The effect was formidable and became part of one's lifelong learning.

Overall, the effect of the experience was that memory was utilized through reflection and recalling, which are part of the *metacognitive processes*. The interconnection of one's reciprocity of thinking and encountering interaction or project-based work for different abilities and ways may well determine the significance of the learning situation's being most positive when one is engaged in it.

Explaining *Affect*

There's much to be related about different ways of implementing learning techniques. The word *affect* means the emotional or feeling sensation impact of something on oneself. When one is referring to the emotional influence of this interactive method/strategy/technique, the first thing that comes to this author's mind is realizing the magnitude and differences of feelings about one's own critical thinking and creativity abilities.

Examples of feelings—in this case, after students were involved in making the self-corrective and interactive Electro-Board—are summarized in the next section. Each student experienced a sense of accomplishment, an emotional reaction of happiness, and a sense of well-being and self-worth. The sensory response was feeling comfortable, like on a spring day when a smile appeared across their face. Learners—and we're all learners—are *effected* and *affected* by circumstances encountered all the time in different locations.

INTERACTIVE INSTRUCTIONAL RESOURCES: ATTRIBUTES

Different ways of instruction bring about five very important qualities referred to as attributes in learners.

- *Ownership:* "This is of my doing and belongs to me and/or those involved in creating something for learning."
- *Self-efficacy:* "I am able to use this to learn a particular topic or use this technique to learn and remember."
- *Empowerment:* "I am enabled, authorized, and permitted to do this work, because of my involvement in it."
- *Self-reliance:* "I am solely dependent on myself. I do not have to call on or go to anyone to discover if my answer is right or wrong. I am independent regarding my success and without seeking approval or being involved in a popularity situation with the teacher or classmates. It's just me using the interactive instructional resource."
- *Self-confidence:* "I'm capable and easily can depend on myself to do what's needed for IBR work and/or required for an assignment that addresses the IM. Making interactive instructional resources is something upon which others may seek my advice, due to my ability to perform and present, knowing I can be relied upon, because of my belief in myself as a capable person."

These attributes take place because, in essence, the student is teaching him- or herself through active participation—muscle memory and brain-based learning and working together, simultaneously, for success. These activities, which are done to create comprehension, involves project and performance-based work. This concept is in direct alignment with Common Core Standards.

JOURNAL AND/OR DISCUSSION QUESTIONS

1. What are the definitions of the Interactive Method, Interactive Book Report, and Activity-Based Learning Centers?
2. What is the overall purpose of the IM and its components?
3. What are four attributes of using interactive instructional resources?

Chapter Five

Memories and Interactive Learning Techniques

This chapter examines memory with respect to involvement in learning, and the brain, the mind, and memories. This information precedes two memory-based narratives about a seven-year old learning to ride a bicycle and a sixth-grade social studies lesson. The three forms/parts of memory as well as the three forms of comprehension are explained, as memory impacts understanding of material that is part of any curriculum, and examples are provided of each type of comprehension. The chapter closes with a discussion of how IBR, ABLC, and P/PBL activities create memories for special needs and different abilities learners.

Some information in this part of this book comes is from the following books where this author has been the lead or only author: *Teaching and Learning: A Model for Academic and Social Cognition* (Schiering et al., 2011), *Learning and Teaching Creative Cognition: The Interactive Book Report* (Schiering, 2015), *Teaching Creative and Critical Thinking: An Interactive Workbook* (Schiering, 2016), and *What's Right with You: An Interactive Character Development Guide* (Schiering, 2017).

LEARNING INVOLVEMENT: REMEMBERING

Before going too far forward, take a look at why this book promotes learning that is based on different abilities, different ways, and special needs. The concept for this, at its baseline, is grounded in forming memory for the retention of information. Later on, this information, regardless of the subject area, may be utilized for life experiences outside of school, such as in a field of work. Then again, one might use this retained information in the classroom, where specified curriculum is encountered and investigations or examinations are given. For this book's writing, that remembering is accomplished through engagement in learning and what it means to be involved actively in the education processes.

Another perspective involving "engagement in learning" is presented in a subliminal or underlying concept by John Dewey as related by Bogner (2011), who discussed how more than fifty years ago, this educational philosopher presented the idea of the relevance of reforming education to make it something to which students could relate both in the present time and in the future. Dewey (1945, p. 50) said, "If I were asked to name the most needed of all reforms in the spirit of education, I should say 'cease conceiving of education as mere preparation for later life and make of it the full meaning of the present.' . . . An activity which does not have worth enough to be carried on for its own sake cannot be very effective preparation for something else."

Addressing students' varied aptitudes and needs is in alignment with that thinking and takes it a step further, as the interaction causes one to remember, and that experience prepares the student for learning most effectively now and later.

Edgar Dale (1946) created a *Cone of Experience* that became popular in the 1960s. As Dale postulated, remembering was realized 10 percent through reading, 20 percent by hearing words, and 30 percent from looking at pictures; however, 50 percent of material was retained by looking at an exhibit, watching a demonstration, or experiencing something happening at a specified location. That 10 through 50 percent of retention was considered to be verbal and visual receiving of information, as learners were being passive recipients of information.

Seventy percent retention was evidenced by participating in a discussion or giving a talk, and the highest level of recall/memory—90 percent—was realized through doing a presentation, simulating the experience, or doing the real thing. Clearly, experience is the best teacher!

Before either Dewey or Dale posited their theories, learning by doing or experiencing was common in apprenticeship programs. Originally related to indentured servitude, this later came in the United States to be known as a traineeship program. This is where master tradespeople in such fields as carpentry, metalwork, gold or silver making, coopering, sheet metal work, or sewing—to a name a few—had people assigned to them practice the trade under supervision. This type of experiential learning—based on the philosophy was that experience is the best teacher—has been common throughout history.

Memory Questions

Are you remembering all that has been presented about the Interactive Method and Interactive Book Reports or Activity-Based Learning Centers up to this point in the book? Each of these activities involve the creation of memory, which deals with how it is formed, what it is like, and why you recall some things and not others.

Important Memory Fact

The first and most important thing about memory is that in order for it to happen, the emotional experience must be significant enough to have one recall it and perhaps even reflect on it.

THE BRAIN, THE MIND, AND MEMORIES

All memory involves thinking—the ability of the brain to process, store, retrieve, and retain information, which is *comprehension*. For example: You receive an invitation to a party. You process the contents of the invitation, with its given date, time, and directions. You either respond immediately or store that information until the deadline for responding has arrived, in which case you have retained, processed, stored, and retrieved information until it could be put into practice. This might be for other assignments or, importantly, for performance on grade-level tests produced by the teacher or a state examination in discipline-specific areas.

TWO MEMORIES

Here are two different situations, one is from my past and the other from my husband's. These situations are remembered to this day, pretty much in their entirety. The involvement in the situation, when they took place, was so strong with a sensitivity/emotional feeling component that the metacognitive processes of recall and reflection were strongly evident.

Age Seven: Riding a Bicycle

When I was seven years old, my dad said he'd teach me how to do this bike riding thing by his holding onto the back of the seat and running alongside my no-training-wheel vehicle. I needed to balance and he'd hold the bike steady. Hesitantly confident, we went into the no-car street in front of our house. I got on the bicycle and began to pedal and steer.

My dad held on to the back of the seat, and I could feel his presence as well as see it from the corner of my eye. Then I pedaled faster. Picking up speed, I was doing well when I suddenly couldn't see my dad running alongside my two-wheeler. Ugh! The handlebars wobbled and turned, and the bicycle ran into the curb. Falling off to the side, I scraped my knee. My dad came running over to me. "What happened?" he asked. "You let go!" I responded through tear-soaked eyes. "How long did you think I'd hold on?" he asked. "Till I was twelve!" I answered.

This was an *emotionally significant experience*. My dad went on to explain that I was doing so well and going so fast that he couldn't keep up with me. He urged me to get back on the bike and try again—with his help—and said that he'd let go at some point but I was to keep pedaling and steering. After several more doing-it-his-way experiences, I then went solo. Once I got my balance, I rode and rode all over the place. Motor memory and brain-based thoughts proliferated. I came to rely on myself for success.

Reflection

I would add that a subliminal message, using recall and reflection, is that I truly didn't want my dad to let go of the bicycle seat and thought his holding on for five years was reasonable. I had come to rely on him as a figure of strength and presence. A long-term result might be that as an adult, I see myself as a responsible person on whom one can rely for the long run—or ride.

Sixth-Grade Social Studies

Over time, our sixth-grade social studies class was to learn about characteristics of each state in the United States, including its shape, size, agriculture advantages, cities, geographic highlights, and so on. Our class was divided into groups, and each group selected from states that were written on slips of paper in a bowl. After this selection we were on our own for information gathering and devising a way to present that to the class.

Our group of six had the state of Indiana. Since we were from New York, this was far enough away from us to provoke some interest. Back then, we used the encyclopedia to gather material; now, one would use the internet for information gathering. (Well, to be fair, we also got a lot of side stories from the aunt of one of the group members, who lived in Indiana.) We made an outline of who would do what and how we would report everything. These things were decided with a vote, as we agreed to make a huge, walkable map of the state using a large piece of plywood or cardboard supplied by one of our parents.

We made nameplates for the key cities in the state—places where different major industries were located, including Elkhart for trailers and motor homes and Gary for steel making. We drew grass and trees on construction paper in different shades of green to represent foliage and glued these to the map. We used other colored paper for landforms and water and other geological features. One of us was really good at three-dimensional construction, so she made buildings and labeled them with the industry name.

We placed all these items in a box that had a template of the state's interior and exterior parts, such as what states bordered it for the outside part and the aforementioned constructions for the inside parts. When it came time for us to do our report, we put our state on the floor and proceeded to tell about each component as we placed it on this floor map. Our classmates were seated on their chairs around us in a circle. As we finished the dissemination of information, the group member whose aunt lived there told a funny story about the corn fields and a scarecrow. This made everyone laugh, and there was an excitement in the room about being able to use the box of state-related objects and put them on the floor map to learn about the state.

Questions

Is there an incident from your childhood—or more recently—that you can recall as impacting your present thinking and/or behavior? If so, what is that experience? If not, what do you suppose is a memory you have that could impact you at a later point in your life? What are some fond memories you have from days, months, or years gone by?

Story Comprehension and Afterthought

When reading these stories and these recollections, the reader, because of the descriptive nature of the examples, may be transported in time to that event or a similar experience. There was the interaction of the main character in two different scenarios. And it was that interaction or activity-based circumstance that caused the storyteller to recall so vividly the events that took place.

I'm confident that all of our Indiana work would be done on the computer nowadays. We'd have matching and placement of tabs with names of cities or places, known as insertions, with the use of the mouse, manipulating what went where on the screen. That is limited interaction, but interaction nonetheless.

However, that interaction back then when I was in sixth grade has created a lifetime of memories. So many of these existed that when we bought a camper and went to Indiana as a family, I was able to tell the kids all about this state before we got there. They thought I was a genius, for which I was willing to take credit. But what I really was equating was being someone who learned by interacting with the group to discover specific facts about this one region of my country.

THREE PARTS OF MEMORY

"The most fundamental things scientists have learned about memory is that we do not store memories whole and therefore do not retrieve them that way either. When we remember something, we actually reconstruct it by combining elements of the original experience" (Brandt, 1999).

Succinctly, the act of remembering occurs in three ways:

1. *Attention:* The ability to focus on a specific stimulus without being distracted.

    Example: We used the IM for the making of task cards for one activity for an IBR. This was in ELA. I made twenty word-opposite matching cards without being interrupted.

2. *Orientation:* The ability to be aware of self and certain realities and facts that manipulate the information. These are commensurate with the ability of a person to respond to stimuli and align with everyday life experiences.

    Example: When making the task cards (see chapter 10) in a small-group format, with five persons each making four cards of word opposites, we noted other groups working on different self-corrective materials. These all were about word opposites, but each group was using a different format. One group did matching on the computer. Overall, I like our group's task card way of doing the word opposites. This is because I can learn from these by manipulating the word and its opposite by matching the shapes, and using them in my own time frame. I am in charge of my learning, and I like that group mates contributed to this activity. We learned from each other by using each other's task cards. I like the collaboration.

3. *Decision making and problem solving*: The ability to understand a problem, generate a solution or two, and evaluate these.

    Example: A teacher candidate explains: "When contemplating whether to use the IM for making word opposite task cards or using the computer for drawing a line to make the match, I decided to use the former. I realized the task cards involved me most in the activity.

    "This task card making helped me learn the word opposites, as well as matching the shape of each card set and knowing my group mates contributed to this endeavor. I learn best when I am fully immersed in an activity, as opposed to minimally engaged or just viewing something. I like the interaction because it helps me retain information. That's why I like the Interactive Book Report so much!"

THREE TYPES OF COMPREHENSION: DEFINITION AND EXAMPLES

There are three types of comprehension:

1. *Literal:* This type of comprehension or understanding is fact-based. The information is gathered from a printed source or first-person experience. The important factor is that there must be a place where the information is available for viewing and that it's factual.
   Example: George Washington was the first president of the United States.
2. *Applied:* This type of comprehension is applied to a personal reaction to a situation. It's how you might or think you would respond or react in the same set of circumstances.
   Example: If I was president of the United States I would feel empowered and try to do the best job for our country. How would you feel?
3. *Implied*: This form of comprehension involves the implication that something actually is about to occur or has taken place. The evidence is indirect, meaning that it's not a fact but is open to interpretation. One is led to believe this is what's going to happen, whether by what was read on some form of media or something witnessed in person. A simplistic way to explain that something is implied is by the context of the material leading one to think what's happened or is about to occur.
   Example: There were bird footprints on the sand at the beach. Since no birds were present when I saw these, it is implied that the birds were there earlier in the day, or maybe sometime in the recent past, but not now.

Now that we have addressed memory and its forms, the types of comprehension, and examples of each, we can begin to understand how using these activities—let alone creating them—causes memories to be formed as the learner is fully and personally involved in the creation or play—the "doing."

MEMORIES AND THE IBR, ABLC, AND P/PBL

Using IBRs, ABLCs, and P/PBL, the IM may involve role-playing, puppetry, or personally made educational games, including floor and wall games. It certainly involves information dissemination in a hands-on fashion, reporting styles, and often persuading others to try different ways of learning. Regardless of the activity, it is the involvement and engagement in it that creates and substantiates memories for later reflection and recall.

What is frequently evident with the IM's components is that there is a presentation of work, such as a project made for display or sharing. Dance and art may be part of these IBR pages, along with any activities, three-dimensional mazes, dioramas, diagrams, drawing, or technology, which are used as tools to assist with these constructions. However, the main components require tactile/kinesthetic as well as auditory and visual involvement in learning, with the use of any or all of the four modalities at the same time. The use of the senses allows for motor and mental memory.

Think about riding a bicycle. What does it feel like? Where are your feet and hands? What's in front of you? What's off to the side? What do you need to do to ride the bicycle? The answer to those questions—whether you've ridden a bicycle recently or twenty years ago—is exactly how the IM works. You remember because you were actively involved in the experience.

And remember, as stated earlier, that this IM of learning and teaching requires as key components *creativity* and *critical thinking*, which form the foundation of any project and/or performance-based teaching and learning for students of different abilities and special needs.

JOURNAL AND/OR DISCUSSION QUESTIONS

1. How is memory involved in learning?
2. What is a memory you have from your childhood, teen years, or adulthood from which you learned something? Explain the situation and how this memory has impacted your life. Next, share your memory with another and ask that person to share a memory with you.
3. What are the three parts of memory and how would you describe each one?
4. What are the three forms of comprehension and what is an example of each one?
5. Why do you suppose that "memories are created" when learners are involved with making or using the Interactive Book Report, Activity-Based Learning Center, or Project/Performance-Based Learning?

Chapter Six

Interactive Learning Technique Pluses, Leadership Building, and Alternative Means of Assessments

The first of the three topics of this short chapter deals with the advantages of utilizing interactive learning techniques when providing instruction. As has been discussed in previous chapters, when it comes to learning, each of us have varied preferences, whether perceptual, emotional, or cognitive. Our preferences often become needs as we rely on what works best for intake and retention of material.

Another part of this chapter, presented by businessman Matthew Schiering, address how utilizing interactive instructional resources as a teaching technique provides for leadership building. Lastly, the use of interactive learning methods as alternative means of assessment to evaluate students' work is discussed.

PLUSSES OF INTERACTIVE LEARNING (SCHIERING, 2015)

Defining *Pluses*, Which Equate with *Advantages*

What do you suppose it means to say that something is a *plus* or an *advantage*? Some might say it's simply a benefit or having a lead over something else, and they'd be correct. Realizing this, physical involvement in learning and teaching definitely serves as the center point of the advantages or pluses regarding this endeavor. In the list that follows, four areas are addressed as being achievements of this project for learners and teachers alike, at any grade or age level. Following this listing, sixteen additional advantages of the IM's IRB, ABLC, and P/PBL are noted.

Four Pluses of the IM's Components

- *Preferred Groupings:* If you're one who prefers working alone or with a partner, in small groups, or on a team, your preferences are met with the IM's IBR, ABLC, and P/PBL. Any group arrangement is possible for the use of this method or the making of instructional resources.

    Things to remember concerning the preferred groupings is that everyone works together to create the activities which are *self-corrective*. This is evidenced by the presence of the answers in the instructional resources or on the back of the activity having the answers, or in a sample of the activity done correctly.
- *Self-reliance:* This is evident when creating any of the IM components because experiential learning is occurring. The makers of an activity come to depend on themselves when designing and creating the project or product and sharing it through a formal presentation.
- *Classroom Community:* The components of IM present an opportunity for classroom togetherness. This sense or feeling of joining comes from working—together or individually—on one of these projects. There is a common goal of creating. Even if one is working to design an activity without the help of others, the final product is shared through the IBR, ABLC, or demonstration/performance of these P/PBL products.

    As many students have shared in their end-of-course reflection papers in paraphrased fashion: I never thought I could work with another person in a small-group format, but this activity of the ABLC had us sharing ideas and modifying them, collaborating on how to make an activity and how it would benefit a student learner. Because we had a common goal and a strong sense of community this project was fun and we learned from it the teaching of building community through interactive educational games.

    This classroom community/sense of belonging occurs when each learner's different abilities and areas of interest are appreciated as part of the common good of the practiced IM. There is an emotional component of enjoying what one is creating, collectively. The making of interactive instructional resources meets and, when completed, fulfills this emotional component of togetherness.
- *Reflective Practitioners and Socialization:* As each of the IM's components is given attention, there is ongoing reference to personal experiences regarding the topic that is being or has been addressed, as well as recalling whether it's from a specific happenstance or situation, or one read or shared as an experience that someone else had. "This reflection and recall is done through the use of memory and, if working on projects with another or others, shared reflection" (Schiering, 2015c, p. 53).

    These recollections help to form ideas for the creation of activities and, of course, the socializing that occurs when there is sharing of thoughts and ideas, and perhaps opinions, judgments, and feelings as well. The final result is *collaboration.*

A component of learning in a classroom—or really anywhere—is that it is a social experience that involves "thinking about one's own thinking" (Olsen, 1995, p. 134). Subsequently, the creators of educational games are socializing reflective practitioners. This being a reflective practitioner means looking back to influence what exactly one is presently, actively doing. Thinking about what one is thinking is *metacognition.*

The cooperation among learners to create something requires ongoing communication. As we already know, learning is not just an academic experience, as there is interaction between individuals through discussion and conversation about the content of material being addressed.

"When working with others, the idea of using one's imagination to create something leads to discourse, both verbally and nonverbally. Conversations tend to expand from the topic of the activity construction to daily thoughts and feelings on happenings. Meaning and perspectives are shared. Information is exchanged and problems are solved in a cooperative manner" (Glatthorn, 1995). This author suggests that this process takes place in the classroom and wherever learning occurs—which is pretty much everywhere!

Perspectives about one's self-image emerge when actively involved in creating an instructional tool. Since, as stated previously, learning is frequently a reflective practitioner process, sharing is colored by individual perspectives, including perspectives about self and others. These come to be recognized as the composition surrounding the social part of learning.

- *Cooperation:* The instructional method interactive strategy calls for learners' cooperating and doing this through discussing, conversing, sharing, prioritizing, examining, evaluating, deciding, informing, synthesizing, conjuring, realizing, risk-taking, comparing and contrasting, classifying, recalling, inventing, imagining, designing, and creating activities to facilitate learning.

The reporting style calls for cooperation as an intrinsic part of the methodology and creation of learning-through-play activities. "With the use of the interaction and acceptance through cooperation, as well as creative thinking ideas regarding oneself and others, the learning community is one that is most favorable for those involved. It's not just cooperation, or community but a comfort zone" (Schiering, 1996).

Culmination of Pluses/Advantage Points

1. For learners, teachers, and everyone involved in the IM or the making of an IBR or ABLC, there is the opportunity to talk *with* one another

as opposed to talking *at* or *to* others. The key expression is talking with, because that involves collaboration and sharing.
2. Individuals, partnerships, or small groups are contributing participants in their own learning, through play and using imagination.
3. Proud ownership of work is evidenced, along with empowerment and self-efficacy.
4. Retention of material is evidenced, because the IM is based on experientialism/constructivism and the end product used as an alternative means of assessment.
5. The nuts and bolts of interactive learning experiences revolve around the design and construction of auditory, visual, tactile, and kinesthetic instructional resources, thus thoroughly involving a sensorimotor and mind approach to learning. The neuroplasticity of the brain is therefore evidenced.
6. Projects may be done individually or provide opportunities for conversation and collaboration, subsequently enhancing *social cognition*.
7. A positive classroom atmosphere is created.
8. Self-valuing is clearly evident.
9. Being a reflective practitioner is emphasized.
10. Work is project- and performance-based, with evidence of the completed work provided in a touchable format.
11. Thinking skills are finitely addressed.
12. No judgments are passed on the quality of work.
13. There is a digesting of one's thought processes and those of others as different pages are played or ABLCs enjoyed.
14. State and Common Core Standards of project- and/or performance-based learning are met and physical evidence is provided.
15. Sharing ideas brings forth trust.
16. Students are teaching and learning from other student learner endeavors while the teacher acts as a facilitator.

Distinctive Consideration

IM, IBR, ABLC, and P/PBL are time consuming. They are projects for both inside and outside of school. If you create them at home to assist you in a specific subject, the making of interactive instructional resources requires concentration. While I do not personally see this as a downside, the fast-paced and/or everything-must-be-done-now society in which we live might define these learning and teaching strategies differently—certainly time consuming, although with tremendous pluses.

LEADERSHIP BUILDING AND INTERACTIVE LEARNING, *MATTHEW SCHIERING*

Let's take a look at leadership with the method and strategy of constant creativity and critical thinking in play. In an article for an internet publication, Matt Schiering (2015) writes about the traits one might possess for this guidance role. His "Leadership Qualities" can be connected to the IM, IBR and ABLC in several ways.

1. *Singularity of Purpose:* These differentiated instruction types for different abilities or special needs students are designed to develop creative cognition through imagining and inventing the pages to be played.
2. *Encouragement, Reassurance, Confidence:* When one is working in a classroom setting or elsewhere at any age/grade level, the overall concept of success is built into the project. This concept is encouraging and provides the desire to continue being creative and use critical thinking skills to imagine and invent activities, because of the triumphant experience being supportive of one's efforts!

    In advance of working on these interactive resources, whether alone or with another or others, the idea is encouraged that this IM attached to the IBR or ABLC can be accomplished. Examples provided by the teacher build self-confidence. When one is working with others, discussion ensues, and this allows for assurance and support of ideas and inventions. This promotion serves to encourage endeavors of varied types of thinking applications.
3. *Collaboration and Reassurance:* Presenting ideas and images in a linear or reciprocal format for others allows for their input. Assistance may be given and cooperation builds strength in purpose.
4. *Optimism:* The invented activities promote and support positive thinking with the idea that this making of pages/learning through play can be accomplished.
5. *Good Planning:* The activities are designed to address varied disciplines. Therefore, the connection between the topics of the pages to be reviewed, learned, or taught must be subject to comprehension of them. This requires preparation and arrangement, as well as sequencing for a wide-ranging and inclusive scope of the project.
6. *Persistence:* Whether one is involved in the IM or making an IBR or ABLC by oneself or with a partner or even in a small group, there is an end product that needs to be presented. This requires goal setting and working to complete the project, which encourages continually moving forward with purpose to produce or reach a goal.

Biggest Plus

It is important to remember: "If you're the user of this Interactive Method and ultimately the *designer* and *creator* of an IBR or an ABLC, then you are the owner. Once you are in possession of something, it's yours, you created it, and your invention becomes valuable because it is of your own making" (Schiering & Marino, 2016).

ALTERNATIVE MEANS OF ASSESSMENT

Throughout this chapter the phrase *alternative means of assessment* has been used. Before addressing this, perhaps it's important to know what is meant by *assessment* and its synonym, *evaluation*. Traditionally, these involve a set of evaluations through questions and answers that may be in any of the following formats: multiple choice, short answer, fill-in-the-blank, column-matching, or small/short essay. Other traditional means include checklists and rubrics.

These assessments may be "[f]ormative, which means they're given throughout the learning process, as this type of evaluation seeks to determine how students are progressing through a certain learning goal." On the other hand, "[s]ummative assessments are given at the end of the year or culmination of a unit of study. Summative assessments evaluate a student's mastery of a topic 'after' instruction has occurred" (Edudemic, 2015).

Formative or Summative Evaluation for the IM?

For the IM and its components presented in this book, both formative and summative assessments may be applied after use of the IM's components. The IBR and ABLC, as well as P/PBL are means or learning tools that result in students doing well on tests. But, overall, these interactive instructional devices call for learners to engage themselves in learning by being involved in educational game construction and/or playing.

The evaluation is done through *observation* of the individual's involvement with the making or playing of educational games, or by the individual separating the known from the unknown in a series of activities, or by an authority figure's watching of the learner's ability to process information, store it, and manipulate or create it to his/her advantage for retention of information.

CLOSING

This presentation of the advantages or pluses of the IM instructional modes, as well as their connection leadership building, is to expose you to different instructional concepts juxtaposed with traditional learning and teaching and assessment. Generally, there is nonconformity with interactive instruction.

I hope you are refining your understanding of new ways to teach lessons and/or concretize those interactive ones of which you were previously aware. Teaching is an art and a craft that encompasses learning—or learning what is best for our students by realizing the many components of meeting the varied aptitudes of our students. As we teach, we learn. And as the next chapter explains, when we use interactive instructional as a form of differentiation of instruction, we are teaching thinking.

JOURNAL AND/OR DISCUSSION QUESTIONS

1. What are five advantages of using the Interactive Method with Interactive Book Reports or Activity-Based Learning Centers?
2. What are three leadership building components of the IM?
3. What are four types of traditional assessment?
4. What are formative, summative, and alternative means of assessment?

Chapter Seven

The Reciprocity of Thinking

This chapter and the two that follow are devoted to explaining the Reciprocal Thinking Phases (Schiering, 1999), the reciprocity of thinking, and definitions of thinking skills, with examples of each one. Specifically, this chapter provides an explanation of each phase, with an understanding of how to teach thinking with the use of interactive instructional resources. Pre-language thinking and evidence of this are given attention.

To fully address the concept of interactive learning techniques this chapter includes an introduction, illustration, definition, explanation, and means of implementation and application of the Reciprocal Thinking Phases for teaching thinking in varied ways. At its core this chapter and the next are about how thinking is seen as hierarchical. However, the author explains that thinking is also a simultaneous process that occurs, consciously and unconsciously, within and between the phases. This is considered to be a reciprocal process.

The phases are: Beginning Awareness (Initial thinking), Critical and Creative Thinking (Intermediate thinking), and the Metacognitive Processes (Higher-order thinking), which is considered the most complex level of thought. An example is provided that uses storytelling to show the aforementioned movement of thinking within and between the three phases. For the Creative portion of phase 2 on the Reciprocal Thinking Chart, Linear and Reciprocal Creative Thinking figures are provided with an explanation.

AN INVITATION TO REFLECT

You're invited to reflect by looking back on your elementary years of learning. If you can, go back before that time. What do you remember? How did you best learn? I can recall the style of presentation of the material to be learned being the same for all students, in the same time period and with assigned seats in a classroom. Desks were in rows and all subject matter was structured. Using one's imagination was not necessarily an instructional factor.

Dissemination of material, regardless of the discipline, was teacher driven. If the teacher didn't like you, life was not easy but if there was acceptance then things were fine. Extra assistance, if you needed it, was in a push-in or pull-out program, but maybe there was a classroom "helper" assigned to assist you. Students may have had different abilities, but different ways were not necessarily addressed. The structure of the classroom didn't automatically accommodate that.

It is often said that teachers teach the way they were taught, and in many cases that may be correct. If that is the case, then educators mostly use direct instruction, a very popular way of teaching in which the teacher is the only controlling person in the classroom.

If the direct instruction method didn't work for the student who later became a teacher, then what? The concept of student engagement in the learning process involves the teacher as a facilitator, not the sole disseminator of information. When the teacher is a facilitator, the students then have a say in how they learn, and in that vein, they become the teachers of themselves; or, with shared responsibility, the students may teach one another; or the teacher may act as both a facilitator *and* direct instruction practitioner. The main thing is there is more than one way practiced in dissemination of information.

You are invited to think about how you like to learn. What's the best way for you to comprehend material that's part of a curriculum? Do you prefer memorizing by reading alone, or learning in groups or in a partnership? Do you like project-based learning? Are creativity and interaction important to you? Where do you like to learn: at home, in school, at the beach, at the library? What time of day do you think you're most attentive? And what do you suppose causes you to remember things you are supposed to learn?

Overall, each of us has our own learning preferences. Each of us has different abilities of one sort or another, because we are all different and do not learn in the same fashion. In today's situation, differentiation of instruction/different ways is what's "in," both intellectually and emotionally. And if it's not "in" where you are, then this book provides ways for teaching strategies to achieve that status.

TEACHING THINKING AND GENERAL THOUGHTS ON THINKING

Have you ever wondered how to teach thinking or when it's being taught? Different abilities and different ways, as presented in the previous chapters, all come down to the teaching of thinking. This is accomplished by giving attention to special needs through differentiated instruction and Response to Intervention and Individualized Education Programs (discussed in chapter 2), as well as the Interactive Method, the use of varied interactive resources resulting in project and/or performance-based work.

The truth is, we're always thinking, but identification of what we're thinking is frequently bypassed as a non-necessity, something we don't address to ourselves or others. Actually, it's like *not* thinking about what one is thinking. Still, we are always thinking, even while resting—although sometimes, especially in the school setting, we're concentrating on the printed words and the message being conveyed.

Consider this: We are not, in fact, accustomed to thinking about what we are thinking. For example, you might see a picture of friends on Instagram and think, "They look good." That's it. You give no thought to what the people are thinking, why the picture was taken, what brought them to that location, or where they next traveled. If anything, we are told what to think, sometimes instructed to ask ourselves what we are thinking, or told *not* to think. Since what we think and feel becomes what we say and do, this segment is devoted to identifying and knowing what you're thinking and how to teach thinking.

Can you read and answer any or most of the comprehension questions asked of you on a given day about what you're reading or about other topics? The answer to those questions deals with the magnitude of evidence regarding your thinking. Being able to relate what you're thinking in an intelligible manner also is indicative of thinking, as you say what's on your mind. So how does knowing what you're thinking matter?

The answer to that is if a person knows his or her thinking process or skills, this knowledge can be put to use frequently and can serve as an empowering agent for self-awareness and realizing self-worth. Subsequently, the teaching of thinking crosses over from the academic cognitive area to the social cognitive one. The experiences that shape our lives are a result of what has been and is thought.

One's ability in school relies on being able to think, to make decisions, to analyze what one hears. Knowing what they are thinking enables individuals to direct their energies toward using their own modifications of viewpoints and to understand which thinking skills to employ to create or use a project, or to conduct a performance that informs and enlightens.

Chapter 7

PRE-LANGUAGE THINKING

What is the evidence of thinking, and do you have it before the acquisition of language? The evidence of thinking is realized in your response to situations: your actions or the things you say or the movements you make.

Here is an example: A toddler is crawling along the clean floor when he sees a toy car. Ask anyone to guess what the child does with the car and the answer will be, "Puts it in his mouth." That's what is done, has been done, and will continue to be done, because the child has had the experience of eating more than anything else, up to this point.

The toy car feels rough and uncomfortable, and so the toddler removes it from his mouth. This action shows there is evaluation going on, possibly comparing the feel of the toy car to other things he's eaten or felt in his mouth. Certainly, there is a recognition that the toy car feels uncomfortable, and by removing it from his mouth he is relieving that discomfort.

A few feet away is a marshmallow, and, coming upon that, the child grabs it and puts it in his mouth. However, this time the object looks okay, feels smooth, and tastes good—so he consumes it right there on the spot, no questions asked.

At this juncture you are asked a question as to what thinking took place on the part of the child with respect to consuming the marshmallow.

RECIPROCAL THINKING: PRE-LANGUAGE EVIDENCE

Evidence of the child's thinking is where the Reciprocal Thinking Phases skills come into play with respect to pre-language cognition. By observing the toddler with the toy car, you witnessed *decision making* as the child put the object in his mouth. Before that, when he first came upon the car, there may have been *recognizing* that it was something to be tried for eating. Certainly, there was *evaluation* of the object in the toddler's mouth as not feeling good, and *advanced deciding* was evidenced by removing the toy car and continuing toward the marshmallow.

The child *takes a risk* in putting this new object into his mouth, but *realizing* it feels and tastes good and *comparing* it to the toy car, he *prioritizes* by mouthing it for *evaluative* purposes and then, completing this *analyzing* while *recalling* the toy car wasn't so good, he eats the marshmallow, which demonstrates his *self-actuating*. Notice that the toddler went through at least one thinking skill in each phase and did it spontaneously. Observing all these cognitive and metacognitive skills is relatively easy for the adult to do, and while doing it, the adult is involved in *analyzing* the situation and possibly *communicating* with someone else what has been observed, much as I am doing now.

The process of observation is important in order to teach thinking, but more important is knowledge of the phases of thinking shown in figure 7.1 and how the skills within this figure apply to thinking through identification by taking cognitive processes to a high level.

The IM and accompanying techniques serve as a constant for the act of recalling, using one's memory, and having experiential learning that results in retention of material. In turn, this retention of material connects with making and using that retention. It's used for the teaching of thinking, through realization that specific cognitive and metacognitive skills are being utilized when activities are being made or played. The mind-brain connection functions alongside tactile and kinesthetic involvement, which involves muscle memory.

THINKING PHASES: HIERARCHICAL AND RECIPROCAL

It is important to note that the Reciprocal Thinking Phases displayed two processes. The first or most easily seen is the *hierarchical* one: movement goes in stages from Beginning Awareness to Critical and Creative Thinking to Metacognitive Processes. This is done to specifically illustrate that some

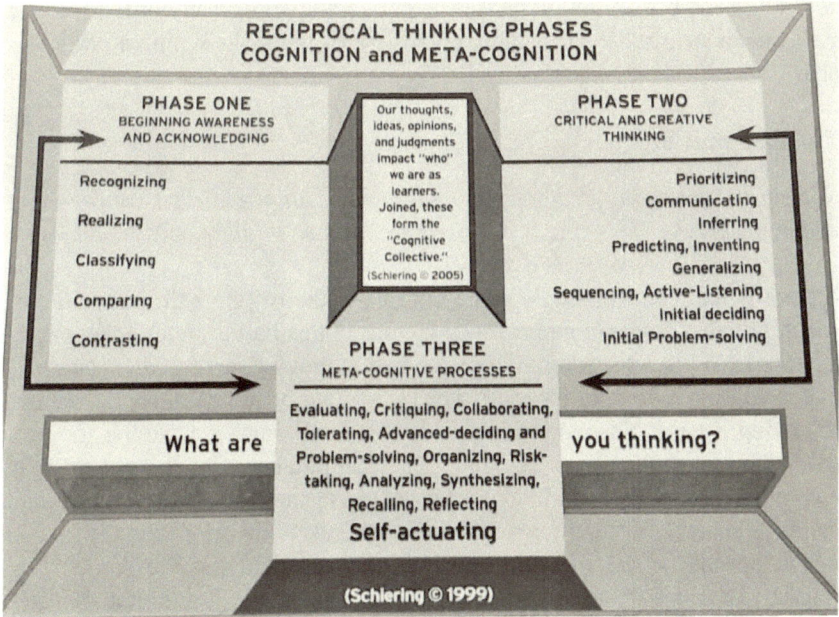

Figure 7.1. Reciprocal Thinking Phases

thinking skills are of a higher order than others, and this movement shows a distinction in the magnitude of thinking going from a common set of skills to more complex or higher-order thinking. The second process, which is done simultaneously with the first process, requires some explanation, as this is the *reciprocal* one. This means that thinking takes place concurrently and instantaneously *within* and *between* phases; there is no set age, stage, or developmental experience that occurs prior to one phase or another.

EXPLANATION THE CONCEPT OF RECIPROCITY OF THINKING

Detail: Reciprocal Thinking versus Hierarchical Thinking

The concept of *reciprocal thinking* was first set forth in 2003 when I moved away from the idea that thinking skills, as I had been taught previously, *only* evolved from one level to another depending on one's experiences. As stated earlier, this is commonly referred to as *hierarchical thinking*. This thinking philosophy, put forth in most educational teacher training, means that thinking moves from one point to another depending on one's age or stage of development; basically, you can't go to a higher level of thinking until you've experienced a lower level of thinking.

This move away from the philosophy of leveled thinking resulted in the concept of reciprocity of thinking: that regardless of experiences, one thinks not in just one phase, but *all* phases, experiencing all or many of the skills at the same or nearly the same time, regardless of the skills within a particular phase.

The Red Ball Story

Note in the following example the movement within and then between and within the phases. Thinking is done reciprocally or simultaneously.

As one is realizing (phase 1) something like "the rolling ball is red," he or she might also compare and contrast (phase 1) this ball to other ones, evaluate (phase 3) the direction in which the ball is moving, and predict (phase 2) that it will move toward the wall. The movement of the ball may be seen as following a particular pattern/sequence (phase 2), such as leaving the person's hands to go toward the wall. Then, simultaneously, the person may recognize (phase 1) the ball as not belonging to the person letting it go and classify (phase 1) different types of these spheres while prioritizing (phase 2) which one he or she likes the most. If the person doing the recognizing (phase 1) decides (phases 2 and 3) to take a risk (phase 3) and grab the ball, he or she may or may not be okay with others observing such an action.

Assignment

As you read the Red Ball story and noted the movement of thinking, you were probably comparing and contrasting (phase 1) some experience you had that would illustrate this reciprocity of thinking. See if you can, working alone or with another, create a story using and identifying various thinking skills in the three phases.

INTRODUCING THE RECIPROCAL THINKING PHASES

Overall Definition: Explaining Phases

The reciprocity of thinking refers to the ongoing exchange of comprehension that forms memory. This exchange occurs within and between the phases of Beginning Awareness, Critical and Creative Thinking, and Metacognitive Processes, as seen in figure 7.1. What you are thinking may not be what I am thinking, but awareness of what is transpiring, cognitively, empowers learners and teachers alike. Knowing what one is thinking helps to clarify learning with the individual's acknowledging the finite identification of the cognitive and metacognitive skills being experienced at any time.

The use of the word *reciprocal* in the name Reciprocal Thinking Phases demonstrates that the processes of cognition and metacognition occur simultaneously (at the same time) as opposed to developmentally (with one evolving from the other). The use of the word *reciprocal* emphasizes that thinking is ongoing and conducted within and between the phases. The movement between and within phases occurs naturally, as one does not purposefully go from one thinking skill to another—it just happens. With respect to the IBR, the beauty of these named and defined skills is in the individual's identification of what one is thinking.

I think; therefore, I am.

Explaining Phase 1: Basic Awareness and Acknowledging

This first phase involves skill development related to fact finding and ordering techniques that include initial classifying, causing the learner to start making connections to personal experiences and those presented orally or in written formats. Learners are able to respond to various stimuli in conversations, as well as to configure answers to literal comprehension questions with accuracy. This phase takes into consideration an individual's earliest forms of awareness.

Explaining Phase 2: Critical and Creative Thinking

The second phase involves transcendence and inclusion through movement from and within one's beginning awareness, as much as within and between the third phase. In this second phase, learners process skills through visualizing and verbalizing the connections they have made from personal prior experiences and/or things they have read or heard from others. It can be determined that the combination of critical and creative thinking relies on past awareness to construct new meaning.

The learner may hypothesize, imagine, or visualize, making connections from his or her own experiences or reading material for applied comprehension. Subsequently, determining outcomes from actions taken provides a comprehensive set of thoughts for initial problem solving and/or decision making. There is also discernment with critical thinking, as well as predicting, and initial decision making by not accepting an answer or idea at face value. One final thing about this second phase is that its name—Critical and Creative Thinking—when analyzed, connotes that in order to be creative, one must employ critical thinking on an ongoing basis.

Personal Perspectives on Creativity and Critical Thinking: Phase 2

I have personally experienced that there is an extensive amount of cognitive and metacognitive skill disbursement during creativity, but not necessarily on the topic at hand. One might recognize a lack of focus when actually a good deal of deep thinking is occurring on the part of the creative person.

For example, a moment of creativity or creation of something may occur when in a classroom, talking with a friend, or being in a small group or alone. Imagine that in one of these situations (except the last), the topic of a historical event is being discussed, with a few questions to follow. The individual in the state of being creative is thinking most seriously about something other than the questions being presented. This may be thinking about music to be composed related to the event, with a melody running through one's mind, or a poem and rhyming verse having to do with that topic—or it may be unrelated to the topic entirely: thoughts about going swimming, or about a painting just begun and how it is to be completed. In this situation, a great deal of thinking is happening, but not necessarily on the subject being presented.

Another example, given by artist Maritza Garcia, explains what happens to her when painting. "My mind stops. Well, it doesn't really stop, as it is concentrating solely on the painting and nothing else. I'm critically thinking about what I'm painting and nothing interferes while in the process of doing that" (Garcia, 2012).

Types of Creative Thinking: Linear and Reciprocal Processes

Most simplistically stated, the difference between thinking that is linear and thinking that is reciprocal is illustrated in figures 7.2 and 7.3, respectively. Each is part of phase 2, which involves not just *creative* thinking but *critical* thinking as well. As seen in figure 7.1 the skills realized in this phase involve prioritizing, communicating, inferring, active listening, inventing, predicting, generalizing, sequencing, and initial deciding and problem solving.

With linear creativity there is movement forward from a beginning to an ending point. There is no moving back and forth between the sequencing; rather, there is a distinct pattern from the first function to the last one, without any variation. The pattern is structured and progressive (Schiering and Byrne, 2016).

However, where there is reciprocity in creativity there is a continual back and forth that may occur at any juncture. One may have an idea, develop that idea, and then go back and change the initial idea to impact the design of what's being created. The flow is not sequential; in fact, it couldn't be more opposite, as often the processing of ideas and the result of that processing to the point of actually creating something occur simultaneously (Schiering and Marino, 2016).

Explaining Phase 3: Metacognitive Processes

The third phase occurs when thinking goes beyond the cognitive and the learner actually knows what he or she wants to realize—exhibiting control over his or her intake of material. This phase involves critiquing accompanied by self-actuation through evaluation and synoptic exercises (general and summative overviews), and a realization of actions that need to be taken to facilitate the acquisition of knowledge. Metacognition is domain dependent,

---

Images/Ideas → Imaginations → Bringing-forth Memories →

Visualizations → and discernment → Sensory responses →

Inventions → Decision-making and → Critiquing →

Problem Solving → Creating

Figure 7.2. Linear Creativity

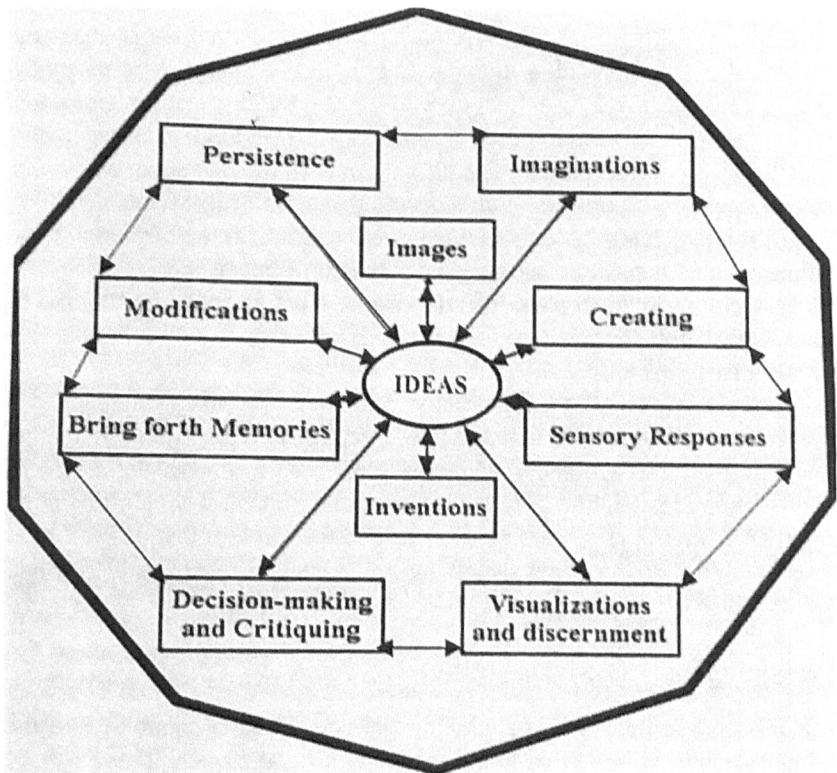

Figure 7.3. Reciprocal Creativity

as it is instantiated (firmly grounded) in a context or learning task (Tobias & Everson, 1995).

This "being grounded" refers to learning that addresses a specific subject area and references students working in a format that is structured and sequential. Abedi and O'Neil (1996) define metacognition as consisting of strategies for planning, monitoring, or self-checking cognitive/affective strategies and self-awareness.

The result of learners and teachers identifying and implementing the higher-order thinking skills in this phase is clearly evident in their ability to ask and answer questions related to *implied comprehension*. This is where the answer is made obvious through conjecture or context clues that lead one to think that a specific answer is viable; for example, in the sentence "I saw a dog's footprints in the sand," it is implied that a dog had previously walked on the sand, because of the footprints. Implied comprehension is based on context clues or illustrative material presented in auditory, visual, tactile, or kinesthetic formats.

THINKING PHASES: EXPLAINING RECIPROCITY

Now that you have seen figure 7.1 and read about each phase, it is important to reiterate that the figure represents two thinking practices. The first or most easily seen is the hierarchical one, in which movement goes in stages between low, intermediate, and high levels of thinking. With this visualization or supposition, it would appear that one thinks in stages and can't go to a higher level of thinking until he or she has experienced a lower level. But that is not the case for the reciprocity of thinking!

The second part, not so easily seen or imagined, is the simultaneous processing of information, in which thinking takes place concurrently and instantaneously *within* and *between* phases. There is *no* set age, stage, or developmental experience that occurs prior to one phase or another, and movement between the phases is fluid.

JOURNAL AND/OR DISCUSSION QUESTIONS

1. What is meant by the idea of *teaching thinking*?
2. How would you explain the new concept of *reciprocity of thinking*?
3. What is a summary, thinking in terms of phases, of the story example you gave?
4. How would you briefly explain the purpose of each phase?
5. What is the difference between linear and reciprocal creativity?

Chapter Eight

The Cognitive Collective

Thinking and Feeling

In this chapter, thinking and feeling are joined together with the term *Cognitive Collective*. The difference between thoughts, ideas, opinions, judgments, and feelings is examined. This "distinguishing one from the other" is presented with a way to test whether you are expressing a feeling or a thought. The reciprocity of thinking is explained in detail with examples of how to ascertain the thinking skills used in a particular situation. Feelings are then addressed using the same situation.

The chapter continues with a discussion of the complexity of thinking and iteration of how thinking occurs within and between phases. Addressed next is connecting one's own thinking with use of the Reciprocal Thinking Phases Skills and feelings to determine, when using IM interactive resources, what specific thinking skills are used when playing a page of the IBR. This is followed by a few final thoughts on thinking and feelings.

THE COGNITIVE COLLECTIVE

Human beings think as well as feel, and this unity of thinking and feeling happens both within the classroom and outside of it. Throughout an individual's day, he or she will move between varying cognitive processes and emotions. As teachers, we must address this natural progression and interplay by recognizing, first, that they occur, and, second, that in order to be effective teachers, we must know how this process happens and attend to it. The Cognitive Collective is the interplay between and within an individual's or group's thinking and feelings.

Defining Thoughts, Ideas, Opinions, Judgments, and Feelings

Reciprocal thinking includes the thoughts, ideas, opinions, judgments, and feelings everyone has that result in a continual structuring and restructuring of their reality—in other words, the beliefs and values upon which they take action. This is accomplished through personal and shared reflection. Reflection is the second highest level of thinking, with self-actuating—taking action—being the highest. For a clear understanding of thinking and feelings, they are defined (Schiering and Bogner 2008; 2011) as follows:

1. *Thoughts:* Immediate conscious responses to reflection, which involve memory. Reflection is further defined by Schon (1997) as having two forms: reflection "in" action, or thoughts occurring now in the present; and reflection "on" action, referencing something that happened in the past. *Example:* From my experience, I have thoughts that focus on learning as multidimensional.
2. *Ideas:* Predictions about future responses or speculation based on one's perspective as a result of reflection. *Example:* She thought about what she'd read and got an idea about good teaching practices as something on which she'd focus.
3. *Opinions:* Combinations of thoughts and ideas resulting in a formulated concept. *Example:* The teachers were asked their reaction to the curriculum and gave a two-page written response regarding the importance of student engagement in learning.
4. *Judgments:* Concretized thoughts, ideas, and opinions that are impacted by memory, while being based on reflection concerning past experiences. Often based on one's level of attachment to a situation, judgments are not easily changed, but they may well change. If they are easily modified, then you've expressed a thought, idea, or opinion as opposed to a judgment. *Example:* My judgment concerning eye color is that green is the most attractive.
5. *Feelings:* Sensory and/or emotional responses, which may be descriptive or classificatory, to stimuli. *Example:* The water felt soft as it slid through my open fingers.

    Feelings are also defined as being a quality in something that evokes a response that connotes feeling of an emotional or intuitive nature and/or reflects on something to establish a formed response that is grounded in thought, ideas, opinions, and judgments. *Example:* The music collectively evoked the audience's strong sense of joy as the symphony began.

    Subsequently, feelings and emotions are one and the same and yet can be observed or defined as being joined. These, then, are transrational responses to stimuli in that a sensory response to a situation occurs at the same juncture as deeply held thoughts, ideas, opinions, and judgments. Bogner & Schiering (2007) refer to feelings and emotions as being "root responses" to stimuli.

In some instances, it's important to note that thinking and feelings are so interwoven, it's difficult to separate one from the other.

Distinguishing Thinking from Feeling

Most times, a person's thoughts are intermingled with feelings such that one is not distinguishable from the other, or they're thought to be one and the same. People say, "I feel that this is good," and it's accepted as a feeling, while it is also a thought. If one examines these *thinking* and *feeling* terms closely, it's discernable that thinking and feeling are separate entities that may also be experienced simultaneously.

The way to differentiate between thoughts, ideas, opinions, judgements, and feelings about something is to use this simple test: If you can substitute the words "I am" for "I feel" and the sentence makes sense, then you have expressed a feeling. If it does not make sense, it is most likely a part of thinking.

Thoughts or Feelings?

- I feel that you should go to the store.
- I feel that this is a happy time.
- I feel these shoes are just perfect for me.

What you see above are three thoughts or opinions, but not necessarily feelings. Let's take the same statements and put them as feelings. They read as follows:

- I feel comfortable with you going to the store.
- I feel happy at this time.
- I feel satisfied that these shoes are perfect for me.

In each of these second set of statements addressing the three original statements, the words "I am" can be comfortably and correctly substituted for the words "I feel." The statement makes sense with either of these phrases, which makes the statement a feeling as opposed to a thought.

Movement of Thinking and Feeling

It is essential to comprehend, literally and through application of the Reciprocal Thinking Phases, that one does not move from phase to phase or experience thinking skills attributed only to the lowest level and then move to higher-order thinking based on experiences, age, or stage of development. Each of us does thinking, simultaneously and reciprocally, within and between lower- and higher-level thinking and accompanying feelings.

Movement of Thinking and Feeling: The Flower Example

Many years ago I was invited to a fellow teacher's home to witness the opening of the flower called night-blooming cereus. I was told—and found it difficult to believe—that this flower blossomed at midnight and stayed open less than twenty-four hours, and moreover, that this flower blossomed only once a year. Subsequently, I took a risk (phase 3) to see if this information was true. As it turned out, the fragrance of this flower was so intense that I still remember it, and it has served as the catalyst for the following example of the reciprocity of thinking and feeling.

Thinking

When looking at the flower, one would be *realizing* (phase 1) this is a flower and at the same moment *analyzing* (phase 3) the shape, color, smell, or details about the flower. What kind of flower it is evidences *comparing* and *contrasting* (phase 1) the flower's nuances to other observed and/or known flowers. One would be *evaluating* (phase 3) whether the flower was liked or not, at the same time *prioritizing* (phase 2) is evident through the reaction (thinking and feeling) to it. *Evaluation* (phase 3) of the color and smell of the flower would take place when *initially deciding* (phase 2) if it is a preferred or favored type of flower.

One can easily ascertain by noting what is in parentheses that thinking is not solely a hierarchical process, but is reciprocal in its composition. One moves back and forth between and within the cognitive and metacognitive skills of each phase. There is no particular order to thinking, but rather it is simultaneous and random with regard to which thinking skills are attended to at any given moment. Also consider that, while one is *thinking* about something, so too one has an *emotional* response involving *feelings*.

Feelings

The viewing of the flower evokes a feeling response such as that seeing the flower made the person feel *comfortable* and *happy*. Those emotions were conveyed through facial expressions when viewing the flower and saying "Hmmm." This is implied comprehension, which means this is not directly stated, but it is clear from the response of the viewer and the one watching that response that the reaction was favorable. Basically, all learning has reciprocity of thinking and feelings. Our life experiences—not the number of them, but the actual experience and at any age—impacts our thinking and feelings.

If the emotional/feeling experience is significant, then it will be recalled for a long time to come. And our cognitive and metacognitive abilities and feeling reactions increase in number and depth with the accumulation of our experiences. The toddler's thinking is simplistic in nature, but becomes more complex as he/she matures. That is an example of human nature.

THINKING COMPLEXITY

> Thinking occurs in varying phases of complexity that are reciprocal in nature with the individual's moving seamlessly between and among them. Each individual's thinking can be characterized by a number of specific cognitive skills that can be identified by individuals. This being the case, one can hone and develop these skills, identifying when he or she is using each and becoming more proficient in its usage.
> Tasks for the learner and the teacher, therefore, would seem to be attending directly to helping one "know what he/she is thinking," helping each learner to identify when he or she is using a particular skill and assisting them in developing mastery over it. (Bogner, 2011)

Additionally, thinking certainly involves the act of withholding judgment in order to use past knowledge and experience to find new information, concepts, or conclusions. To think critically, one moves from guessing to estimating, from grouping to classifying, from supposing to hypothesizing and having opinions based on reason. Thinking is truly a complex process.

CONNECTING THINKING AND FEELING TO THE IM

Thinking

Using the IM and an interactive instructional resource/educational game for construction or play leaves one involved with realizing what needs to be done to interact with the project. Examples include: *recognizing* the components to be utilized, manipulated, or put together; *comparing* and *contrasting* this one to others experienced; *classifying* components of the instructional resource; and *prioritizing* what will be facilitated first, second, and so on. One also experiences *making predictions* about the outcome of the project, *communicating* with others as to how to construct or play the game, *synthesizing* the actions taken or thoughts thought, *making a decision* as to what's to be done next, *evaluating* the situation, *deciding* how to make it different or better, and *taking a risk* in deciding to move forward in construction or play.

If you're creating interactive resources, you would add to the previous paragraph the thinking skills of *inferring, inventing, sequencing,* and *generalizing,* which involve critical and creative thinking (phase 2), as well as *advanced problem solving, recalling, reflecting,* and *self-actuating* (phase 3). The overall idea is that you know what you're thinking, and by making and interacting with this type of resource you're continually utilizing thinking skills.

Feeling

Connecting feelings and emotions to the Interactive Method is the result of an individual's emotional reaction to the instructional resource or educational game. Was the user successful with the means of interactive learning? Was there a sense of security, well-being, and ease? These questions need to be answered in the affirmative in order to match feelings with a positive cognitive experience. Even if there is risk taking, the end product may be accomplishment, leaving the individual with a sense of comfort and acceptance.

I have observed that many times—*most* times—one's emotions are in agreement with one's thinking. If there is *decision making* there might be anxiety, but not so much as simply *realizing* and *comparing* and *contrasting.* Overall, if there is success with the learning process, that main sensation is one of security, even relaxation. There are a multitude of emotions one might experience with any type of instructional tool or method. Finding the interactive instructional resources that work best for different abilities is one of the foremost considerations of this book and its companion.

FOUR FINAL THOUGHTS + A POEM

1. Thinking . . . thinking . . . thinking . . . feeling . . . feeling . . . feeling! These, together, are who we are. When? Every day, in every way. Succinctly, we are influenced and defined by what we think and feel. The interesting part is that thinking and feelings change. The Cognitive Collective combines these, and, as such, our common social and societal realities and beliefs and values come to have meaning. With respect to this book, cognitive and metacognitive skills are experienced when making or using interactive instructional resources. (These are presented in a small sample in chapter 10, and many more are included in the companion book.) Then, when we share these activities with those who have different abilities and special needs, we come to join together in teaching and learning using the IM.

   The reciprocal thinking skills illustrated in figure 7.1 are easily demarcated; however, the myriad feelings are not so definable. *Sometimes we need to know that feelings just are . . . they exist.* Regardless, we learn from our emotional, sensory reactions to presented material, and we also learn from the thoughts, ideas, opinions, and judgments we have or others express. The main idea is to learn from what we are thinking, and build upon that for personal awareness and success in the academic and social spectrums.

As one teacher candidate stated, "[T]he active engagement in learning and knowing what cognitive skills were being used brought interest and developed the students' learning abilities. Teaching themselves with self-corrective techniques, student-learners said, made them feel 'smart'" (Spotkov, 2014).

2. When I taught differentiation of instruction and the Reciprocal Thinking Phases skills with the IM, IBR, and ABLCs in South America, the reaction was much the same as in the United States and Europe. There was excitement about being so engaged in teaching and learning. Also, submitting the IBR on the computer made this a technology-based means of instruction, and that exchange of information took interactive learning to a whole new level.

3. In 2016, one teacher candidate commented that although his time in the classroom had been short, he had made clear and distinct observations:

> First I noted that the type of school district is inconsequential, as are the types of students in that district, when it comes to responses to interactive methods (IM) being practiced.
>
> Everyone, including the teachers, enjoys interactive learning. I observed the students and saw what interested them and what made them want to learn. Students experiencing interactive learning, most often and frequently 100% of the time, reacted positively. Knowing what they were thinking was an added plus. (Laupheimer, 2016)

4. The IM and techniques that come with it in this book are a pass-along: giving or paying it forward for differentiation of instruction, adaptable to different ability learners and special needs persons, for ultimately the teaching of thinking that provides comprehension and retention of subject matter effects and affects us all.

Joining Thinking and Feeling

I think . . . therefore I am.
I feel . . . therefore I am.
Where did I learn that?
Perhaps it's not as important as realizing
"What" we think and feel.
By knowing and sharing that
You come to realize who I am
And

> I come to realize who you are.
> The thinking and feelings of each of us
> Create the "you" and "me" of us.
> (Schiering, Summer 2011)

JOURNAL AND/OR DISCUSSION QUESTIONS

1. What are the definitions of *thoughts*, *ideas*, *opinions*, *judgments*, and *feelings*?
2. How is it possible to distinguish expression of a feeling as opposed to a thought?
3. What does the idea of *thinking complexity* entail?
4. What are two final thoughts expressed at the close of the chapter?
5. How would you explain the Cognitive Collective?

Chapter Nine

Definition and Examples of Reciprocal Thinking Phases' Skills

This brief chapter addresses the definition and examples of the Reciprocal Thinking Phases featured in the Reciprocal Thinking Phases Chart found in chapter 7 (figure 7.1) and referenced throughout the book.

DEFINITIONS OF THINKING SKILLS IN THE RECIPROCAL THINKING PHASES

Phase 1: Beginning Awareness and Acknowledging

1. *Recognizing* is the skill that helps a person to be aware of or identify things from previous experience, and also to acknowledge something as being new to the person.
   Example 1: Sue became aware of the person's presence when she was tapped on the shoulder.
   Example 2: The car was shiny and looked brand new.
2. *Realizing* is the skill that helps a person to make real and comprehend the importance of something that he or she did not know previously.
   Example: The participants felt comfortable, for the first time, when everyone joined hands to sing together.
3. *Classifying* is the skill that helps a person to arrange things into groups according to established criteria, such as age, height, color, type of clothing, or some other category.
   Example: There were five apples, three oranges, and two plums next to one another in a line on the table.

4. *Comparing* includes examining or judging two or more things in order to show how they are similar.

    Example: The moon looked the same color tonight as it did last night.
5. *Contrasting* focuses on the differences between two things or more. When you combine comparing and contrasting there is discernment, a distinguishing between one thing and another, or perhaps one idea from another, as to differentiate and perceive.

    Example: The red shoes worn by the first girl were way longer than the brown shoes worn by the second girl in the lineup for music class.

Phase 2: Critical and Creative Thinking

1. *Prioritizing* is the skill that helps a person deal with things in order of their importance.

    Example: The first thing I liked about the class was the way the presenter spoke. The style of delivery was engaging.
2. *Communicating* refers to the exchange of information or conversation with other people using words, signs, or writing. This involves clearly expressing thoughts or feelings so other people understand them.

    Example: The driver yelled out the words on the sign, which read, "No parking here!"
3. *Inferring* is the act of deducing or forming of an opinion based on information one has previously experienced, or indirect evidence that is present.

    Example: The bird prints on the sand let passers-by know that a bird had been on the beach earlier that day.
4. *Active listening* is the skill of being attentive to the point of not just hearing what is being conveyed, but examining it mentally in order to respond beyond simply repeating what was heard.

    Example: The students showed they were attentive to what was being said, and this was evident by their participation in the discussion that followed the presentation.
5. *Inventing* is discovering, thinking up, devising, or fabricating in the mind, thinking out, producing something new, or originating through experiment.

    Example: The student was given credit for originating the idea of a snack time before lunch in the fifth-grade class.
6. *Predicting* is the formation of an opinion that something will happen before it actually has occurred.

    Example: The day was cloudy and gray so people thought there was rain coming soon.

7. *Generalizing* is the formation of an opinion after considering a few examples of the topic being addressed.

   Example: Most people in the room, it was supposed, would accept the free chocolate offered them when attending the school's parent teacher conferences.

8. *Sequencing* is the skill of arranging a series of related events, actions, or the like in a particular order.

   Example: Everyone received a song sheet and then began to sing the song. Next, a few singers harmonized; then the audience applauded, whooped, and cheered because they loved the singing.

9. *Initial deciding* is the preliminary forming of a new idea that might change immediately or in the near future.

   Example: Initially, there were three choices for what school to attend after high school graduation.

10. *Initial problem solving* is finding the correct preliminary answer to a question situation or circumstance or an explanation for something that is difficult to comprehend.

    Example: When the dogs were chasing each other, their owner thought it best to separate them or to have one sit on his lap while the other was under his arm. Either of these ideas could solve the problem at this moment.

Phase 3: Metacognitive Skills

1. *Evaluating* is the skill involved with judging or determining the quality of something, to assess or appraise its worth.

   Example: The estimate for doing the painting was more than the homeowner wanted to pay.

2. *Organizing* is the skill involved with making something into a whole with unified and coherent relationships or arranging thoughts in an orderly fashion, and is sometimes referred to as being logical or sequential.

   Example: The kids cleaned their room by putting the clothes on hangers in the closet and lining up pairs of shoes under the bed while putting sweaters on shelves.

3. *Critiquing* refers to the formation of a thought or judgment as to whether something is good, bad, or somewhere in between. Critiquing may also be an opinion that connotes whether something is favorable, unfavorable, or possesses both of these components.

   Example: The teacher appraised the student's work to be formidable and designated a grade of 94 percent.

4. *Collaborating* is working together with another person or group of people in order to achieve or produce something.

Example: Two students worked together on the final project. They shared their ideas on how this was to look and be presented to the class.

5. *Tolerating* involves a pattern of recognizing and accepting a behavior or situation that is not, in the opinionizer's viewpoint, favorable.

    Example: Although she didn't necessarily want to eat the pie, she did to allow the guests to feel comfortable.

6. *Advanced deciding* involves the processes of reaching a high degree or level of difficulty with respect to a choice, judgment, explanation, and/or resolution to a situation. Such thinking is accomplished by providing clarification about a tough or challenging situation, finding the correct answer to a question, or elucidating something that is complicated, intricate or complex to comprehend.

    Example: The student made the final choice as to how the division problem should be done.

7. *Risk taking* requires grabbing a chance without knowing the outcome.

    Example: They had never been ziplining before, but they decided to be brave and give it a try . . . just this once.

8. *Analyzing* involves the careful examination of something in order to comprehend it, including the examination of thought and feeling components to ascertain their general composition in order to understand them.

    Example: The individual cautiously approached changing the flat tire after intently reading the instruction book on how to do this.

9. *Synthesizing* is forming the events of a situation by bringing together separate parts of a situation in a concise manner.

    Example: The person told a story in five minutes that actually took place over twenty years. She consolidated the events.

10. *Advanced problem solving* involves in-depth analysis of a situation in order to determine a way to handle it.

    Example: After careful and considerable thought, and realizing some ideas were better than others, the dog ate the food on the television tray that its owner had mistakenly left near the couch where the dog was sitting.

11. *Recalling* involves bringing back to one's mind something from the past, as a memory, whether from a moment earlier or a longer expanse of time, in order to address a situation that requires a decision.

    Example: The memory of the snowstorm and getting stuck on the parkway was vividly brought into view when it began to snow yesterday. So the car's driver took a different route home.

12. *Reflecting* is the act of thought or contemplation, often resulting in a realization.

Example: The twins vividly recalled and shared the swimming competition events.

13. *Self-actuating* has to do with going forward and taking action, doing something as opposed to remaining sedentary.

    Example: The dogs ran across the floor with wet paws, causing their owner to mop up their footprints before company came to the house.

What Are You Thinking?

JOURNAL AND/OR DISCUSSION QUESTIONS

1. How would you define each of the three Reciprocal Thinking Phases?
2. Selecting two cognitive skills from each phase, how would you define these?

Part II

Different Ways of Teaching, Personal Commentaries, and the Author's Closing Thoughts

Chapter Ten

IM's Self-Reliance and the "How-To" of Teaching Thinking

This chapter first addresses how the Interactive Method creates good feelings about learning and develops self-reliance. Then, three activities are presented in figures 10.1–10.3, with narratives explaining each one. The explanation of the activities gives attention to thinking skills that are employed when making and thinking about how the activities foster memory acquisition. These activities are a taste of what readers will find in the companion book, which includes numerous narratives and illustrative activities.

IM'S GOOD FEELINGS AND SELF-RELIANCE

When learners are given the freedom to create and think critically, in close proximity to one another, the result is a sense of good feelings about their abilities being evidenced and enjoyed. This concept was presented, as you may recall, near the end of the previous chapter. When you're making an interactive instructional resource, playing one someone else has constructed, or designing and making a project, a sense of self-reliance prevails, along with feelings of accomplishment and emotional exuberance. (At least, all my years of teaching have continually shown this type of reaction.)

Feedback from teacher candidates over the past twenty years has related that this type of hands-on instruction has been helpful because the talk has been walked throughout the semester. (For more on this, see chapter 3 in the companion book.)

INSTRUCTIONAL RESOURCE: DIFFERENT WAYS: TASK CARDS

Task Cards: An Interactive Instructional Resource for Teaching Thinking: *Marie Calder*

One interactive instructional resource presented in detail in the companion book is task cards. Marie Calder (2017) explains these as a shape match activity most commonly involving two puzzle pieces, as shown in figure 10.1. The pieces created using blank 5x8 index cards that are each separated into two pieces by cutting them apart in the center and in different ways. The left and right or top and bottom sides, depending on how the cards are oriented, have the matching question and answer.

There are a multitude of possibilities for using this activity with math equations, decimals, word opposites, nouns, verbs, adjectives, consonant blend words matched with pictures, vocabulary words matched with definitions, geometrical shapes matched with their names, and so on.

The interaction involves putting the pieces together, as the shape matches are different for each set of cards. The Reciprocal Thinking Skills involved are: *recognizing* the topic and different shapes, *comparing* and *contrasting* the sides of the cards and what is on them, *inferring* that the match is correct and the information accurate for the match, *synthesizing* the information into a specific category, *prioritizing* the cards to be matched, *initial* and *advanced deciding* about the answer, *problem solving* by examining the answers when matched and read, *generalizing* that this activity will assist in learning the material either through making the cards or using them, *risk-taking* when the initial match is determined, *evaluating* the answers, and *self-actuating* when the activity is done.

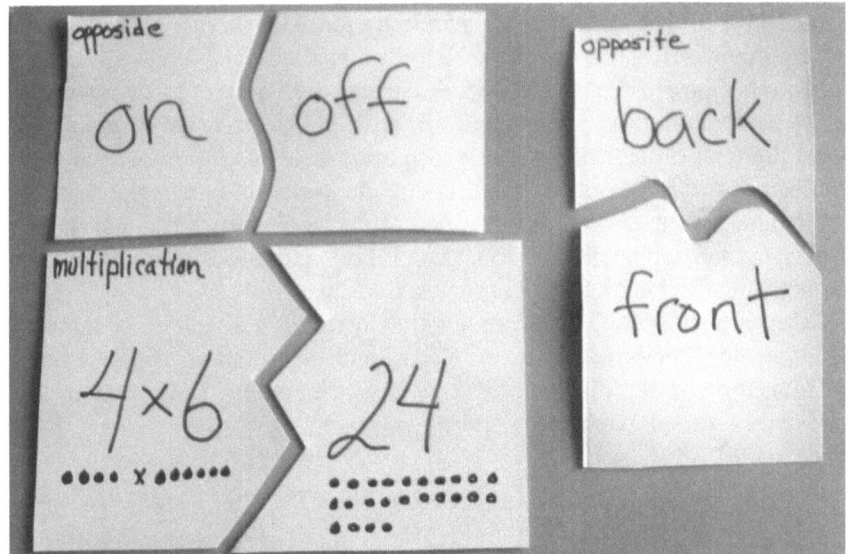

Figure 10.1. Task Cards

INSTRUCTIONAL RESOURCE AND P/PBL DECISION MAKING AND RECIPROCAL THINKING: DECISION-MAKING GRAPHIC ORGANIZER/ DMGO

Combining Critical and Creative Thinking using the IM

In two courses at Molloy College—one an undergraduate English course and the other a graduate reading and language arts course—the topic of decision making has been presented for the past twenty years. Before that, I presented it at the middle school and then the fifth-grade elementary school level. The process one might go through in making a decision is questioned and then analyzed at length, then a method for making a decision by thinking through and designing, then constructing a poster-sized graphic organizer is presented. Most interestingly, many times the topic of the decision-making graphic organizer is one that has to be researched to get information about characters in the story or facts about the subject matter being addressed.

Decision making or problem solving involves finite attention to critical thinking through analysis. Creative thinking skills are used with attention to designing a DMGO. Other thinking skills for this activity given attention are *realizing* the topic, *classifying* the possible positives and negatives, and *comparing* and *contrasting* these.

From phase 2 is *decision making* and then *prioritizing* the importance of each possible positive and negative outcome. *Communicating* is done in written format when viewing the finished DMGO and then when it is presented in a formal manner for a demonstration with discussion about how others might solve this problem. Note that applied comprehension occurs when other possible plus and minus outcomes are shared. *Active listening* takes place during the presentation of the DMGO with listeners *predicting* what the final choice will be. The entire board involves *inventing*, and there is also *generalizing* when those observing the presentation agree or disagree with the ideas presented. *Sequencing* is realized with the layout of the DMGO. Then, too, metacognition is continually addressed, as it occurs when an individual is thinking about his or her thinking.

Basically, this DMGO teaches thinking by using nearly all of the thinking skills on the Reciprocal Thinking Chart, and many others as well. These additional ones might include *differentiating*, *discerning*, and *inductive* and *deductive reasoning*, to name a few.

DMGO COMPONENTS

Notice in figures 10.2 and 10.3 that there is first the statement of the Problem, followed by the naming of three possible solutions: Choice #1, Choice #2, Choice #3, or you could title Choice #3 as Another Idea. Three possible positive outcomes and three possible negative outcomes follow each choice. The reason for the use of the word *possible* is that the decision hasn't been made and the ideas are only likelihoods, as opposed to facts for definite outcomes. The last part of the graphic organizer is the Final Decision and Why. The individual making the board utilizes the possible outcomes, weighs them by prioritizing them, and then states these priorities as the choice and the justification for that choice. Subsequently, what is written on the board is used to show and justify the final decision.

It is very important when using this DMGO process that another option or reason for the final decision is not entered into the mix unless implied by the entries on the board. While one might present other choices and possible positive and negative outcomes on the board, only those on the board are included in the final decision as the reason why. This is done so the thinking procedure, development, progression, method, practice, and manner are evidenced. (In chapter 3 of the companion book, the section "Decision Making: Purposes and Illustration" further explains the concept of this specific graphic organizer or text structure.)

Figure 10.2 shows a DMGO created by Nickolas Marsala in the fall of 2018. The drawings of the superheroes are representative of Marsala's artwork, and each illustration was done freehand. Figure 10.3 shows a DMGO done by Jerry Redondo during the same semester of the same year. Each portion was covered with an acetate sheet cut to match the shape of the section. Three-dimensional stickers or cutouts were placed by each of the choices to let those reading this work identify the career choice with artifacts representative of it.

The Design of the DMGOs

These two graphic organizers, which are sometimes grouped with other ones under the title of "text structure," have been color coordinated. This means that the borders of Choice #1 and its corresponding possible positive and negative outcomes have been done in one color (green), Choice #2 and its corresponding components have been done in a different color (purple), and Choice #3 and its corresponding components have been done in blue. The Problem and Final Decision and Why are done in a fourth matching color to show continuity. This visual effect provides the reader of the DMGOs an easy way to identify the flow of the board's content.

Superhero Choice by Nickolas Marsala

The Text of the DMGO Figure 10.2

Problem: Which Superhero would I want to be if I had the opportunity to become one of them?
   Possible Choices: #1: Spiderman, #2: The Hulk, Another Idea: Green Lantern
   Possible Negatives for Choices: #1: Spiderman isn't bullet proof, isn't knife proof, and Spiderman is vulnerable to what normal human beings are vulnerable to, even with his enhanced senses.
   Possible Negatives for Choice #2: Even a slight outburst of anger or excitement could turn a person into the Hulk, and this uncertainty is stressful for everyday life and would interfere with social and family life.
   Possible Negatives for Another Idea: Green Lantern's weaknesses include the color yellow and lead, something as simple as a number 2 pencil could kill him, in theory, the Green Lantern could hesitate to rescue people because of these flaws/drawbacks.
   Possible Positives for Choice #1: Spiderman has enhanced senses which impress mankind, he can crawl or climb up walls, and Spiderman has super strength and amazing reflexes.
   Possible Positives for Choice #2: The Hulk would be the strongest person on Earth, he would be unstoppable against any force of nature, and because of this strength the Hulk has a powerful ego.
   Possible Positives for Another Idea: Green Lantern's powers come from his ring, so his physical being isn't changed, he can fly, and he can create things with his mind.

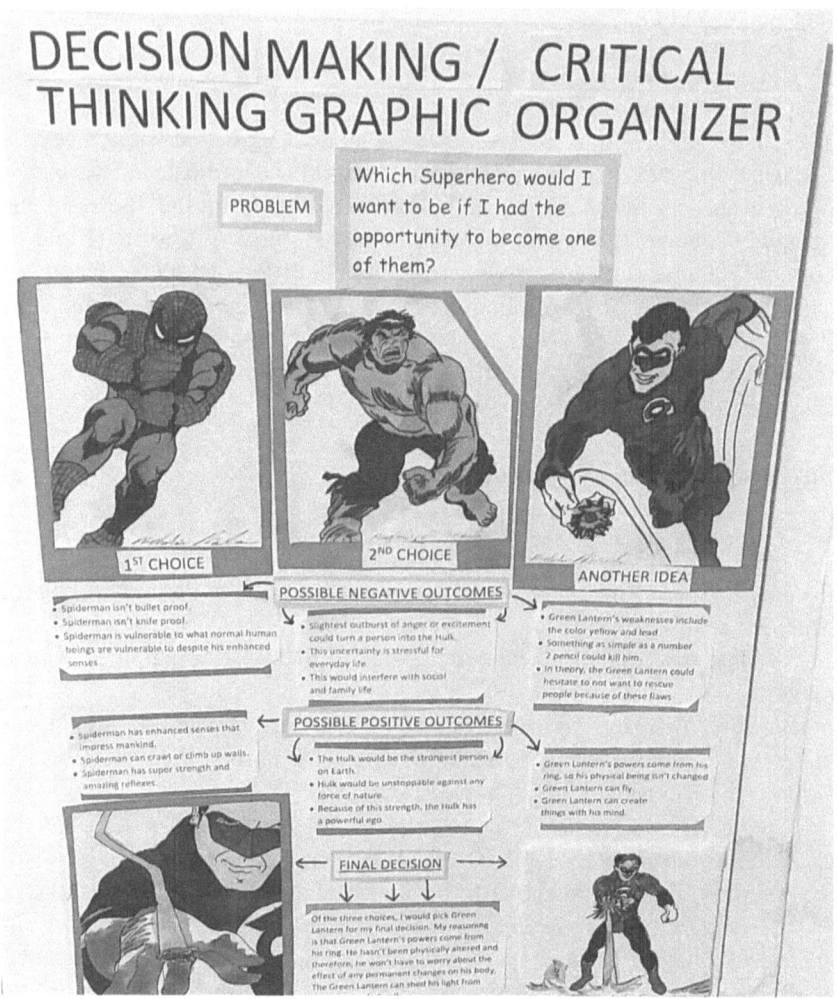

Figure 10.2. Superheroes DMGO

Final Decision and Why: Of the three choices, I would pick Green Lantern for what Superhero I'd want to be. My reasoning is that Green Lantern's powers come from his ring. He hasn't been physically altered and therefore, he won't have to worry about the effect of any permanent changes on his body. The Green Lantern can shed his light from his ring over dark evil.

Career Choice by Jerry Redondo

The Text of the DMGO Figure 10.3

Problem: Where would you like to be in your career five years from now?
   Choices: #1: Firefighter, #2: Teacher/Professor, #3: Police Officer
   Possible Positive Outcomes for Choice #1: Ability to make a positive impact in your community, you'll always have physical conditioning and

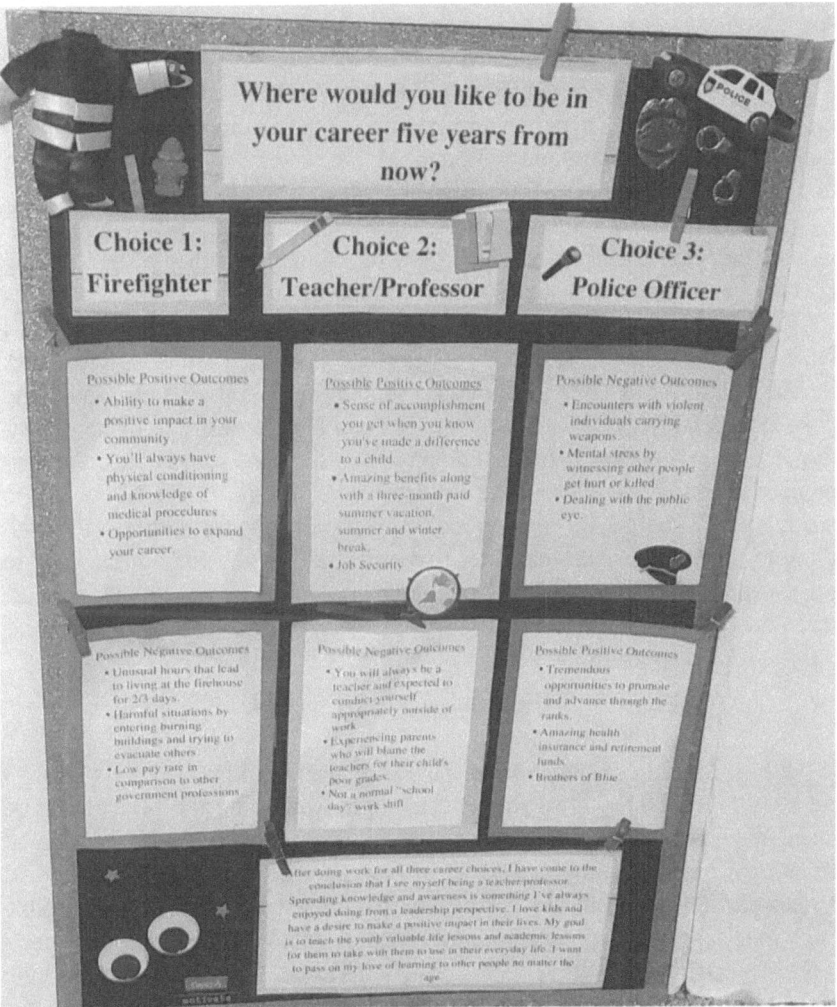

Figure 10.3.   Career Choice DMGO

knowledge of medical procedures, and there are opportunities to expand your career.

Possible Positive Outcomes for Choice #2: Sense of accomplishment you get when you know you've made a difference for a child, amazing benefits with pay distributed/amortized for the whole year, and job security.

Possible Positive Outcomes for Choice #3: Tremendous opportunities to promote and advance through the ranks, amazing health insurance and retirement funds, Brothers of Blue.

Possible Negative Outcomes for Choice #1: Unusual hours that lead to living at the firehouse for 2–3 days a week, harmful situations by entering burning building and trying to evacuate others, and low pay rate in comparison to other government professions.

Possible Negative Outcomes for Choice #2: You will always be a teacher and expected to conduct yourself appropriately outside of work with a high moral code in place, experiencing parents who will blame you for any of their child's poor grades, and not a normal "school day" work shift compared to other professions that go 9:00–5:00.

Possible Negative Outcomes for Choice #3: Encounters with violent individuals carrying weapons, mental stress by witnessing other people getting hurt or even killed, and dealing with the public's eye/opinion

Final Decision and Why: After doing work for all three career choices, I have come to the conclusion that I see myself being a teacher/professor. Spreading knowledge and awareness is something I've always enjoyed doing from a leadership perspective. I love kids and have a desire to make a positive impact in their lives and the community. I'd have a sense of accomplishment in knowing I'd made a positive difference in a child's life. My goal is to teach youth valuable life lessons and academic lessons for them to take with them to use in their everyday life. I want to pass on my love of learning to other people no matter the age. Teaching has amazing benefits and job security.

EXAMPLE OF THE TEACHING OF THINKING: DMGO

What follows is an explanation of the teaching of thinking using the DMGO for the topics of (1) what superhero one might want to be and (2) what future occupation one might choose. As you might already see, the teaching of thinking is ongoing with this DMGO activity. The activity puts the individual maker of the DMGO in the act of thinking about what choices are possible and what possible positives and negatives are plausible before a final decision is reached and written. This act of thinking encompasses one teaching him/herself thinking by being involved in that act of thinking through recognizing and identifying those cognitive skills/thoughts regarding what's to be placed on the DMGO.

The one reading the DMGO is teaching him/herself thinking while going through what's printed on the Organizer and determining if these are the same choices and possibilities, as well as final decision. If not, then ther is more teaching of thinking with how that DMGO topic would be addressed if applicable to that person.

Take a thoughtful look back at the Reciprocal Thinking Skills and their definitions in chapter 9. Then take a look at the next paragraph for a list of thinking skills and their application when doing the DMGOs seen in figures 10.2 and 10.3.

The task of creating the DMGO involves determining the topic problem which involves *realizing* and *recognizing* that three choices. This involves *prioritizing* and *initial decision making*. Then there is an ongoing *comparing* and *contrasting* of these choices with *initial* and later *advanced deciding* to *problem solve* and come to a *final decision*.

The process of doing involves *prioritizing, synthesizing,* and *sequencing* the pluses and minuses; *communicating* with oneself and others regarding what is a best choice (*prioritizing*); *classifying* characteristics of the superheroes or jobs; *evaluating* them; and *sequencing* them for placement on the display board.

Next, is the task of *analyzing* the choices' positives and negatives; *recalling* thoughts, ideas, and opinions about what each superhero or career entails; and exhibiting *advanced problem solving* when making the decision. In the career choice DMGO, this results in *self-actuating* when going forward and doing that teaching, which was the final decision.

When the DMGO is completed and presented to the class there is *communicating* of the thinking that was done by addressing what is in the *sequenced* and *organized* parts of the board. The board designer's and creator's thinking skills are observable, and this brings about *comparing* and *contrasting* one's own ideas on the topic. *Teaching thinking through an interactive instructional resource has been accomplished!*

CLOSING THOUGHTS

This chapter has primarily dealt with the IM as it addresses cognitive awareness, with a few examples. Mainly, the idea is that interactive instructional resources, as represented with the task cards and the P/PBL decision-making graphic organizers, are means for teaching thinking skills through identification and implementation.

JOURNAL AND/OR DISCUSSION QUESTIONS

1. What was related about task cards and the Interactive Method with respect to thinking?
2. What are the components of a decision-making graphic organizer?
3. What is one purpose of a DMGO?

Chapter Eleven

Objectives of the Interactive Method and Its Components

This chapter primarily references one of two of my college courses that use the IM's "different ways" approach to teaching and learning. Overall, this is for the teaching of thinking through active engagement in experiential learning. This chapter outlines the rationale for the IM and its components, as realizing the objectives of lessons leads to achievement of assignments to fulfill goals. It should be noted that although these objectives were designed for a college course, I have used them, in one capacity or another, for discipline-specific assignments conducted throughout my teaching career at various grade levels.

Subsequently, these aims are applicable at *any* grade level for *any* teachers. For student learners, some of these objectives would require a substitution for the topic that is being addressed in the curriculum. An example would be replacing reading methods with a subject area topic, such as "our solar system" in science.

This chapter begins with an invitation to you, the reader, to consider your own teaching style. Then, Molloy College's "Values of a Shared Vision" are listed and defined. This is followed by my objectives when it comes to classroom lessons for one of my college courses; these objectives may be modified to meet curriculum-specific goals that may apply to any grade level from kindergarten through advanced education.

Instructional experiences for each objective that include demonstrating and generating knowledge of student development are provided with regard to all students, including those with different abilities and special needs.

AN INVITATION

You are invited to look at your own teaching, regardless of the setting. How do you do that? Hopefully it is by setting an example of how things are to be done by modeling the lesson to be taught. This is so each student may emulate you and thereby meet with success. That is an overall goal of teaching so that learning is realized at an optimum level.

ACHIEVEMENT OR FAILURE

Do we learn from achievements and accomplishments or from mistakes and failures? I think the former are more applicable than the latter when it comes to how we best learn. However, there is a good deal of rhetoric that relates how individuals overcome failure to achieve. Within each attempt at some lesson there is success, just with the trying.

It's important to offer positives and praise that encourages and lifts learners' spirits. Failure—or a sense of it, or being told one is a failure—truly tends to freeze and thwart learning, often to the point of being so challenging it may be detrimental to learning, and the learners give up trying.

Addressing Achievement

Learning from successes may be a new concept, and acknowledging some accomplishment in each learner's situation might also be a relatively unexamined idea. You are asked to consider the potential of addressing achievement as opposed to what is wrong. You're invited to emphasize what was done and what was accomplished, as opposed to focusing on what wasn't done exactly the way the end goal was envisioned. This vetoing of negativity is so an establishment of creativity or individual differences or varied interpretations of a lesson are the mainstay.

Both before beginning my college professorship and afterward, I practiced modeling lessons or assignments by showing and doing the IM. This was and is because I discovered that when learners were involved in gaining information, they remembered lessons/assignments and were prepared for testing on those lessons.

The following pages address the goals of the IM, drawn from my teaching years in Ohio and North Carolina and New York, and now at the college undergraduate and master's level. This is first accomplished through elucidation and explanation of the college's shared vision statements, followed by the objectives of experiential teaching and learning, with an explanation of each one.

VALUES OF A SHARED VISION

One of the first portions of the reading and language arts course—or, for that matter, any course at Molloy College—is the shared vision of the institution. The following is a portion of what these courses first address. Exclusive to the courses I teach is that the Interactive Method addresses each of these visions with the explanation that follows the bulleted terms. The overall attitude concerning these visions is that we are here to learn from one another; we are, in a sense, "one" in our goals and aspirations; each person is a teacher and learner simultaneously; and we are joined together in a sharing community of educators for practice and lesson-incorporation of not putting anyone down, but lifting spirits to have a sense of self-worth and acceptance of self and one another.

- *Belief that all children can learn:* The emphasis of this statement is on the word *all*. This refers to the idea that if there are students in the classroom who have learning differences, different abilities, or some special needs that require differentiation of instruction and different ways, there is still learning that can be accomplished, because each individual—whether there is a difference related to culture, age, religion, ethnicity, aptitude, processing style (and the list goes on)—can learn.
- *Learner-centered and value-centered curriculum and pedagogy:* This refers to lessons being designed for students, as opposed to a teacher-focused learning environment. Values relate to the importance of beliefs, morals, ideals, tenets, standards, and principles that bring us together for the betterment of our classroom community. There is not a competition determining who is good, better, or best, but rather placing importance on a pedagogy that addresses good.
- *Ethics and spirituality:* Ethics deals with morals, integrity, principles, and conscience as part of one's demeanor and behavior when in a classroom setting that promotes a sense of togetherness for the common good of all. For most, spirituality refers to belief in a higher power; an appropriate synonym would be piety.
- *Intellectual curiosity:* The pursuit of this shared vision would be to have lessons that are scholarly and arouse one's interest and inquisitiveness.
- *Independence and risk-taking, while promoting collective identity and responsibility:* The practice of freedom in lessons is done with the idea of providing lessons that have learners use their imagination and creative abilities while taking a chance at exploring a new idea, and joining together with others in a camaraderie that supports an allegiance to the group, with each one being aware of the similarities of purpose and character being of a positive nature. Respect, caring, responsibility, trustworthiness,

kindness, good citizenship, and fairness would be the operatives for such a learning environment.
- *Diversity, multiculturalism, and pluralism, including divergent thinking:* The first of these is addressed with attention to the different abilities of students who come from culturally varied backgrounds and a respect for those differences being evident with a predominant attitude of positivity in the classroom. Heterogeneity is commonplace in the classroom with thinking exhibited and accepted that is not closed, but may be opposite from others.
- *Passion for teaching:* This refers to an educational setting where educators exhibit a desire to be in that setting. Such an attitude or demeanor is opposite of one that relates, "I'm here for a paycheck," instead relating, "I'm here because I have a love of this profession and the children in my charge."
- *Commitment to students and their communities:* For the most part, this is a classroom that has lessons demonstrating dedication to values and skills that include a desire to succeed, a sense of the lasting importance of learning, and belief in each one's ability to learn.
- *Civic responsibility through the promotion of social justice and interdependence:* These refer to the addressing of public concerns and promoting community with the idea of being fair (everyone getting what he or she needs) while promoting reliance upon one another: student-to-student and teacher-to-student (and vice versa).
- *Commitment to democracy:* Dedication to the concept that all members of the community or, in this case, the classroom community, have a say in its governance.

OBJECTIVES OF A SIX-CREDIT COLLEGE COURSE IN ELA

The following objectives were applied to a college course in English language arts. However, these goals of lessons may be applied to any grade level, and to students with varied abilities. This is accomplished by substituting the assignment to be done in your classroom in place of the specific assignment listed for the ELA class.

Course Rationale

1. *Demonstrate* an understanding of the philosophical and sociological foundations of education, the content areas to be taught, and translate these understandings into *effective teaching* through understanding and implementation of the following:

a. Student processing style with respect to brain dominance, if any, and preferences regarding modalities, room design, working with other or alone, intake, time of day, level of illumination, structure, persistence and other components of the Dunn and Dunn Learning Style Model (1976–2008). And, varied instructional strategies in the integrated language arts. These objectives may be modified to interdisciplinary methods or children's literature courses for the diverse learner's classroom;
b. Attention to the constructivist theory with implementation of differentiated instructional methodology and using the Interactive Method of teaching and learning.

2. *Develop* lessons employing appropriate content and pedagogical practices that support instruction, including the use of research, reflection, and technology through:

   a. *Evaluation* of pedagogical approaches for the integration of the language arts in contexts while addressing teacher candidates' literacy history;
   b. *Discussing* diverse learners' needs in the development of thought and language with attention to diagnostic teaching of reading, writing, listening and speaking;
   c. *Designing* a literature-rich learning environment with emphasis on Schiering's Reciprocal Thinking Phases: Cognition and Metacognition (1999). These are hierarchical and simultaneous processes with (1) cognitive skills identification, (2) management of the academic environment, and (3) instructional strategies that pertain to students with diverse abilities in the inclusion or mainstream classroom;
   d. *Identifying and comparing* the beginning and emergent reader;
   e. *Analyzing* for the purpose of decision making about problematic situations or ones requiring intensive thinking to formulate thoughts, ideas, opinions, and judgments, as well as feelings about topics that impact one in the social cognitive areas;
   f. *Modeling* through the professor's instruction and then teacher candidate research the meaning-through-reading techniques with utilization of strategies. Each reading method includes the following requirements:

   - *Individual and Qualitative Reading Inventories (IRI/QRI) for diagnosis and assessment* ** (This is the first of six additional methods to be taught through a teacher candidate reading method packet, which has evidence of detailed explanations of the reading method, and a one-page tri-fold brochure that evidences key points of the method to be addressed. Both the packet and brochure need to have a minimum of four references. Lastly, there is a demonstration lesson of the designated reading method).

Specifically, the administering of an IRI and QRI allows the teacher to be aware of reading difficulties, reading level, and the impact of these on comprehension and/or decoding, as well as oral and silent reading showing evidence of a reading problem such as word transposition, omission, interjection, and/or substitution of words. (Additionally, evaluation of the IRI and/or QRI course assignment provides the teacher with information on which reading methods are best suited for individual student learners). Each of the following reading methods are addressed:

- *Guided Reading*;
- *Shared Reading*;
- *Phonics, Phonemes, and Decoding Strategies*;
- *Reciprocal Reading*;
- *Readers' and Writers' Workshops*; and
- *Balanced Literacy* (This reading method is presented last when doing the reading method packet, brochure and demonstration lesson. This is because this BL method has many of the other reading methods in it. Reading aloud and choral reading are usually the ones not previously addressed and may be used for the requirements of the demonstration lesson).

g. *Demonstrating*, through oral and written language, the following:

　a. Effective teacher-student conferencing;
　b. Development of reading and writing as reciprocal processes;
　c. Construction of graphic organizers for reading lessons involving critical thinking and decision making, as evidenced in the Common Core Learning Standards and those of NYS, as well as CAEP, INTASC, and ACEI standards;

d. Exhibiting storytelling that promotes critical analysis with emphasis on Beginning Awareness and Acknowledging, Critical and Creative Thinking, and the Metacognitive Processes, as presented in the Reciprocal Thinking Phases. Also, convergent and divergent questions should be addressed that are extensions of the storyline.

h. *Configuring instruction* for student learners that demonstrates knowledge and practical application of:

   a. How to design a reading lesson in oral and written formats;
   b. Interdisciplinary and interactive tri-fold boards for in-class childhood instruction (optional).

i. *Generating various types of writing techniques for purpose and form*, which include, but may not be exclusive to:

- Connections with children's literature;
- Strategies for differentiated instruction;
- Team Learning and/or Circle of Knowledge (The first of these involves reading a short story and answering literal comprehension questions about it. Then, there is one requirement involving creativity. This might be writing a poem about the story or doing a drawing or role-play. The second, Circle of Knowledge, involves collaboration with having one minute to list all the words associated with a topic, such as ecosystems, pioneers, or outer space exploration: grade-level curriculum specific. A point is attributed to each word as long as there are no repetitions);
- Organization;
- Goal setting;
- Problem solving;
- Prewriting, drafting, revising, editing, while sharing/publishing, and student grouping.

j. *Formulating and self-actuating* research-based instructional strategies, through the presentations/demonstrations of interactive lessons in reading, English language arts, and which may incorporate reading in the content areas within the presentation.

3. *Provide instructional experiences* that result in active student engagement with appropriate classroom interactions, meaningful use of technology, instructional materials and resources, and student attainment of the learning and professional standards through:

   - Designing and teacher candidate presenting/modeling of reading and writing lessons;
   - Designing, constructing, and presentation of interactive instructional resources;
   - Developing questioning techniques that correspond to thinking phases for student learner cognitive/metacognitive development in the areas of awareness, comparison and contrast, critical and creative thinking, reflection, problem solving, prioritizing, recalling, risk-taking, tolerating, and self-actuating;
   - Utilizing the storytelling experience for writing, speaking, and listening;
   - Designing an author study via the Interactive Book Report (IBR) with *technological* components;
   - Presenting and teacher candidate assessment of small-group folktales in a literature/book talk format;
   - Analyzing content-area reading and strategies to promote student learner excellence in *literal*, *applied*, and *implied* interpretive comprehension areas.

4. *Demonstrate and generate* knowledge of student development, and appreciation of diversity, and application of developmentally appropriate instructional strategies for the benefit of all students, including students with different abilities and special needs, by addressing "differentiation" of instruction and "adaptations" for student learners.

   This is to be accomplished through partnership presentations regarding the reading/writing, strategies, programs, and/or institutional techniques presently utilized for learning-different students in the inclusive classroom. These include but are not specific to:

   a. Reading and/or writing disability
   b. ADD and ADHD
   c. Dyslexia
   d. Physically impaired
   e. Emotionally problematic or classified mental illness
   f. Gifted
   g. OCD
   h. Any listed special needs from chapter 2

(Further learning-different students criteria is located in the appendices of Schiering, Bogner, & Buli-Holmberg, 2011).

5. *Implement* various types of formal and informal assessment techniques to measure student learning and make appropriate modifications and interventions based on assessment results:

- Recognizing varied means of assessment (summative and formative: multiple choice, matching, fill-in-the-blank, short answer, essay, educational gaming) and student evaluation techniques that are in accordance with lesson plan objectives and NYS learning standards, with adherence to a multimodality approach; Common Core application;
- Addressing a cognitive or learning-style inventory.

6. *Develop effective collaborative relationships* with students and their parents, with support personnel, and with the community by attending PTA meetings, or related organizations where pertinent topics are addressed. A mock parent-teacher conference with the professor and a colleague will be role-played in our class to facilitate parent/teacher roles. The following topics will be for classroom discussion during this course:

- Analyzing parent-teacher conferencing role-play for impact it may have on the student and within school relationships between parent-teacher and student;
- Discussing expectations for the teacher candidate in the assigned school observational and participation experience;
- Discussing and analyzing the role of the new teacher, with respect to interpersonal and intrapersonal communication in the school environment;
- Discussing and analyzing the role of the teacher with respect to the school and community as impacted by personal beliefs, personal/school/student values, socialization techniques, placement (grade-level), and experience in teaching;
- Addressing birth through grade two reading lists;
- Role of Common Core learning standards in the school; and
- Discussing the New York State's Dignity for All Students Act (DASA) content material, following attendance at this mandated certification professional meeting.

7. *Develop a personal philosophy of education* that serves as a basis for professional decisions and reflective practice, using portfolios, research tools, and scholarship for ongoing growth and improvement.

- Analysis of the teacher-candidate cognitive style inventory;
- Writing a personal literacy history with comparison through sharing with peers' literacy history;
- Writing a philosophy of education statement to be included in teacher candidates' personal journals for use in developing this narrative during student teaching;
- Interviewing a teacher and/or past or present professor for comparison of viewpoints involving perspectives of educational philosophy and changing perceptions, teachers as agents of change in the classroom, present-day issues impacting education in the collegiate, private, and public sectors. These are done with journaling chapter questions that appear later in this syllabus.

8. *The designing of text structures/graphic organizers* that include at least three of these as presented individually and/or are in an IBR: Descriptive Maps, Story Maps, Character Analysis, Problem solving/ Decision making, Sequence of Events, and Cause and Effect. (These graphic organizers/text structures are discussed in detail in chapter 9).

JOURNAL AND/OR DISCUSSION QUESTIONS

1. What, in your opinion, are the most important shared visions?
2. Of the listed objectives of this college course, which are three of greatest importance to you, and how would you implement these in your classroom?

Chapter Twelve

Two Personal Perspectives Addressing Special Education

This chapter is rather unique in that it first provides research on special education and then offers a personal perspective regarding experiences with the contributor's own different abilities child. Maggie Blair, auxiliary assistant professor at Molloy College, offers the first narrative, and Kevin Cooney the second.

DISABILITIES, DIFFERENCES, AND DIVERSITY, *MAGGIE BLAIR*

Defining Disability

What is a *disability*? Might this word appear to be defined the same as *different* when viewed through the lens of learning style, perceptual preferences, or other components such as those who prefer room accommodations, sound present, or high illumination, along with other preferences mentioned in chapter 3 of this book? Might students classified with a disability share common instructional needs with students who are culturally and/or linguistically diverse? These are questions I now ask after spending more than thirty-five years in the field of special education.

Current research on communities like the Deaf community and the emerging autistic culture clearly indicate that today. many successful as well as young members of these communities no longer think of, or refer to themselves as, individuals who have a *disability*. They instead view themselves as *diverse* members of the human community.

Along this same line of thinking, there are many current and well-respected researchers in the fields of dyslexia and ADHD who are now most likely to employ the terms *different* or *diverse* to describe their research subjects. The current research is, however, slowly but definitively chipping away at the previously established boundaries that corralled students into labeled categories and away from their typically developing peers.

Some History

In the past, *dyslexia* and *ADHD* were terms frequently found in the lexicon of disabilities. Is this current movement merely a change in terminology, or is it a significant realization that disabilities may, in fact, represent differences and/or diversity within the human condition? The more significant question, however, is: "What effects might this current movement has on the field of education?"

The prefix of the word *disability* derives from the Latin root *dis*, meaning "not" or "absence of" some cognitive function. Hence the literal interpretation of the word *disability* means "absence of ability." According to *Webster's II New Riverside Dictionary* (1996), to *disable* means to "incapacitate or to make powerless."

As defined by the Americans with Disability Act, "A person with a disability is a person who has physical or mental impairment that substantially limits one or more major life activities, a person who has a history or record of such impairment, or a person who is perceived by others as having such an impairment" (ADA, 2009).

Rights of the Disabled

The Individuals with Disability Education Act (IDEA 1990, 2004) explains that a child with a disability means:

> A child evaluated in accordance with Sec. Sec. 300.304 through 300.311 as having one or more of the following:
>
> - mental retardation,
> - a hearing impairment (including deafness),
> - a speech or language impairment,
> - a visual impairment (including blindness),
> - a serious emotional disturbance (referred to in this part as "emotional disturbance"),
> - an orthopedic impairment,
> - autism,
> - a traumatic brain injury,
> - another health-related impairment,
> - a specified learning disability,
> - deaf-blindness, or
> - Multiple disabilities.

These individuals, by reason thereof, require special education and related services.

IDEA: Definition of Classification

The IDEA definition was designed to be a legal definition and therefore contains functional language, thus making it appear to be the least negative of the aforementioned definitions. However, the IDEA definition specifically identifies the eligibility process for potential special education services. This process mandates a comprehensive evaluation.

The purpose of this evaluation is to identify specific areas of deficit in order for a student to access special education services. Therefore, the entire focus of this evaluation process is, in fact, deficit analysis. This type of analysis identifies the "dis-abilities" as opposed to different abilities of the student, to aligning the "dis-abilities" to a classification.

The next step in this process is addressing the "dis-abilities" through goals and accommodations/modifications listed on the student's Individualized Education Program. In addition to mandated modifications and accommodations, *Teaching and Learning: A Model for Academic and Social Cognition* (Schiering et al., 2011) explains, "This is where differentiation of instruction comes into play by providing instruction that meets the needs of the individual student."

Deficit-Driven Codification

In *Neurodiversity in the Classroom*, Thomas Armstrong, PhD, (2012) cautions that "[t]he process of negotiating an IEP focuses exclusively on addressing a child's deficits at the expense of focusing on strengths that teachers could employ to engage the child's interests and help build confidence." While the eligibility process for special education services was put into place to ensure that all students have access to free, appropriate public education, my interpretation of this quotation finds it evident, then, that the eligibility process for special education services is clearly a deficit-driven process.

The Education for All Handicapped Children Act (1973), IDEA (1990), and the IDEA Reauthorizations (1997, 2004) codified the special education eligibility process and ensured access to supports and services for individuals with disabilities. What might be the impact of a change in terminology from *disability* to *difference* or *diversity* on ensuring accessible learning environments for individuals who are currently covered under IDEA?

The Deaf Community: Disability Codification

Difference or Diversity: The Deaf Community

One way to begin a discussion on *disability* versus *difference* or *diversity* is to look to the one group that, although covered under IDEA, has had a long and rich history of viewing themselves as different or diverse: the Deaf community. This community in the United States dates as far back as 1854, when 1 in 155 residents living on Martha's Vineyard were deaf. In her 1985 book *Everyone Here Spoke Sign Language*, Nora Ellen Groce explains how Vineyarders who were born deaf were fully integrated into the community and were not seen—nor did they see themselves—as disabled.

During the 1980s the group Deaf Pride united and solidified deaf advocacy and ultimately defined this community. In 1988, students attending Gallaudet University successfully protested the appointment of a hearing president during the Deaf President Now movement. These students closed the university and marched on Washington, DC. The students' efforts resulted in the appointment of I. King Jordan as the first Deaf college president (Introduction to Contemporary Special Education: New Horizons, 2014).

Deaf Linx (n.d.) is a website that provides current resources for deafness, Deaf culture, and American Sign Language (ASL). It was originally created by Amy Frasu and is currently run by Donna Robinson, MS Ed, and Ericka Wiggins, MS Ed. The professionals behind Deaf Linx believe that "deafness is not a disability, but a condition that produces a sub-culture that should be celebrated." Therefore, members of this specified culture do not see themselves as disabled, and resent any discrimination or inference that they are disadvantaged. They have a physiological difference but do not see that as anything negative or that should be changed.

Autism, Dyslexia, and ADHD: Disabilities or Neurodiversities?

Autism

In *NeuroTribes: The Legacy of Autism and the Future of Neurodiversity*, Steve Silberman (2015) acknowledges the legacy and impact of the community on the development of the "autistic culture." Through his extensive and in-depth research on the history of autism, particularly current trends within the autistic community, Silberman developed a very convincing argument that autism should not be identified as a "disability" but rather, following the lead of young, successful autistic individuals, that autism represents differences between and among humans and is a part of the human condition.

Dyslexia

When they published *The Dyslexic Advantage: Unlocking the Hidden Potential of the Dyslexic Brain*, Drs. Brock and Fernette Eide (2011) introduced the terms *dyslexia-related abilities* and *dyslexic advantage*. This groundbreaking book expanded the possibility that dyslexia is much more than a disability. The authors defined dyslexia in terms of differences and diverse abilities, noting that these differences existed between dyslexic and nondyslexic brains.

The authors defined terms *dyslexia-related abilities* and *dyslexic advantage* as "the remarkable abilities that individuals with dyslexia commonly possess—abilities that appear to arise from the same variations in brain structure, function, and development that give rise to dyslexic challenges with literacy, language, and learning" (Eide & Eide, 2011).

Like autism, dyslexia is another variation in human development. Should dyslexia be considered a *disability* or a *difference*? What do you think? From an educational standpoint, dyslexia is defined by the National Institute of Child Health and Development (n.d.) "as being a specific learning '*disability*' that is *neurological* in origin . . . characterized by *difficulties* resulting in *deficits* that produce *secondary consequences* and additional *impairments*."

Based on the research completed by the Eides (2011), the challenges encountered by dyslexics in the areas of literacy and language have been the "exclusive focus of dyslexic research and education." The Eides' research, however, took another path. They looked at dyslexia from the perspective of *learning or processing style.* Subsequently, their work may have identified another group who are more diverse than disabled. Through their extensive review of brain structure and function research, these individuals have successfully linked with other current researchers to explain why dyslexics process information differently.

ADHD: Diverse or Different?

Another group of different learners who may also be more *diverse* than *disabled* is those individuals diagnosed with attention deficite hyperactivity disorder. This group of individuals is probably the largest group, because often the autistic spectrum and dyslexic individuals also have comorbid diagnoses of ADHD. In 1995 Thomas Armstrong published *The Myth of the ADD Child.* In this groundbreaking book, Armstrong introduced a new way to view children profiled with attention and behavior challenges. In the book's preface, he raised questions about the focus of research occurring at that time. He indicated that the narrow lens of the research on causality and links to brain abnormality overshadowed the possible examination of the value of neurological differences.

In his later work *The Power of Neurodiversity: Unleashing the Advantages of Your Differently Wired Brain* (2011), Armstrong identified eight principles of neurodiversity. Two of these principles focused attention on the concepts of *diversity* versus *difference*. Principle 2 states that "human brains exist along continuums of competence. And, it is suggested that all humans are somewhere along continuums related to literacy, sociability, attention, learning and other cognitive abilities rather than separated into *normal* and *those having a disability*" (American Institute for Learning and Human Development, n.d.).

Principle 3 is very insightful as it explains that "human competence is defined by values of the culture to which you belong" (American Institute for Learning and Human Development, n.d.). Armstrong explains this principle via societal and cultural values and codifies this opinion by looking at dyslexia. He points out that "150 years ago, dyslexia was unknown" (American Institute for Learning and Human Development, n.d.); however, today, students are labeled "dyslexic" based on "the social value that everyone is able to read by a specified time or at all. This thought concludes that "diagnostic categories are not purely scientifically-based but reflect these deeper social biases" (American Institute for Learning and Human Development, n.d.).

Summation: Disabilities versus Differentiation

Through current brain-based research and the pioneering work of individuals who were identified as disabled, we are now more aware of differences in brain structure and the impact those differences can make of a child's success in the classroom and in life. By viewing a child through the lens of *neurodiversity* as opposed to the lens of *disability*, we come to appreciate the entity of the whole child, both his or her challenges as well as his or her unique talents and strengths.

According to Armstrong (2017), "By using the concept of neurodiversity to account for individual neurological differences, we create a discourse whereby labeled people may be seen in terms of their strengths as well as their weaknesses." He also stated that when innovative terminology is introduced and effectively employed in professional conversations, paradigms can change.

Author's Perspective: Closing Comments

I question whether we currently are on the verge of a major change in education. In my opinion, with more professional dialogue focused on diversity and difference and less dialogue focused on disability, we, as educators, can enhance classroom experiences for everyone. We can empower children to learn their own way, to take personal pride in their accomplishments, to be active members in the learning process, and to make significant contributions as adults to society.

AUTISM AWARENESS: INTERVIEWING A DIFFERENT ABILITIES CHILD'S PARENT, *KEVIN COONEY*

The Present

I've heard it said that experience is the best teacher, and I think that might be true. My wife and I became aware of and knowledgeable about special needs and different abilities with our at-home reality of raising our daughter. Colleen is now twenty-two years old. She lives with my wife and me. She's a lovely young woman. She doesn't speak. She is our joy, and we love her and want others to do that as well.

It has been a journey to raise our daughter. We have voyaged a path we'd not intended to take and weren't ready for, or, at best, were ill-prepared to travel. But we did just that! In the process we learned, specifically, about what it is to be autistic. We learned about the social stigma many experience with this type of situation, not just from a parent's perspective, but from what we think is our child's perspective as well.

Some might see our life with our now-adult child as lonely. But they don't know, nor does anyone know, from our perspective, what they haven't lived. Yes, there is empathy, which is close, but still not the real thing. We are concerned about our daughter's future because we don't know how long we'll be around to provide a safe haven for her.

Overall, that is what we want: a place of comfort and compatibility for her in her surroundings. For example, Colleen works now, and has for some time, at a hotel chain as one who cares for the rooms' linens and neatness. She comes home from work, has a snack, colors, eats her dinner, and watches television before going to bed and repeating the same routine the next day. There's security in having a pattern of activities. Colleen smiles beautifully, and we are her main source of caregiving.

The Past Two Decades

As I reflect on the past two decades and two years, a lot of thoughts about what has been experienced come to mind. Colleen had and still does have sensory integration problems, and my wife and I didn't originally know that was part of autism. We learned that 1 out of 36 has autism today, but it was 1 out of 300 back when our daughter was diagnosed by a neurologist. My knowledge was limited to having seen the movie *Rainman*. When she was two years old, I was terrified as to what would become of her. And so I did my best to block my mind from this problem. My goal became to find a cure.

I wanted something to make our daughter perfectly well. I heard about a medicine from pig's intestine, but blocked that thought.

My wife and I joined a support group and discovered that the negativity in it was more than we could tolerate. They talked about the governance, and who had power and who didn't. At home, our little girl went for walks with us. Before that, she crawled around the house. We attended classes to find out about the spectrum, and we prayed she'd talk and the doctors would be wrong. We got her intervention, which was a good thing.

Since I knew there was a social disgrace or humiliation back then, and perhaps we feared being part of that with our only child, we got involved in autism awareness. My search was focused on what our daughter *could* do instead of what *couldn't* be done. My wife's focus was finding therapists and managing a schedule of services, and both of us felt as though we were struggling to get through each day, caught between what we knew and didn't know, what could be done and did work, and what might not work. There was a preponderance of questions twenty-plus years ago. Maybe less was known *then*?

Colleen rode the bus to where services could be provided, and it was forty-five minutes from our house—a long ride for a young child. Then there was an ABA (autistic behaioral analyst) provided, and this program brought rewards for what our daughter could do. Success at putting a square block in an opening that matched the shape was one thing. Moving a penny—and we did this in the house—was another thing rewarded. Truthfully, saying there was so much success sometimes seemed so small.

Looking back, we see that our girl never got to be a kid. She was always working at one task or another, rather than doing the fun things one associates with childhood. (What will happen to her when we're gone? Day-hab? A group home?) In those early years, we blamed ourselves for her problems and we were secretive about them. Colleen didn't socialize. Speech, if there at all, was murmuring words, and we were happy she wasn't a wanderer. We observed that sometimes things she could do one day, she couldn't do the next. We wondered if the skill set would return. It was baffling, but we noted that she could, at the very least, follow simple directions as they were given. And a routine could be followed.

A bright side to our daughter's autism is that she has receptive language! She has an iPad with a speaker and uses it in school and at home. She points and can do some signing and has a few skills. At age two, she had a fifty-word vocabulary that was lost by age three, and nobody knew why. *What caused all this?* we questioned.

We were told it wasn't a vaccination and it wasn't the environment from which she was having this autistic reaction. So what was it? What it was and has been is an unanswered question. And what gets done is dealing and living with not having answers, but trying to find ways for her to live comfortably among a community of others who are not as challenged as she is.

Small things become important. We watched our daughter progress and realized she's very vulnerable because she has no speech. Her abilities are inconsistent; she is able to do something one day, but not the next. And with this, a big concern is that there's no one to rely on when we're not with her. Yet our community, her teachers, know she's loved and that's a form of protection. Colleen had an IEP, and it was used without guarantees and no specified accountability if she didn't reach a goal. But at least she had one. When you have a special needs child with different abilities, the smallest thing can be huge when it comes to teaching and learning.

What's the magic formula for our daughter? There is none. We shaped our life and belief and value system with her. Material things became far less important, and service headed any list as the thing held in highest value was human development. So if you ask what is most important to us as parents, it's that our adult child be treated with respect and dignity, love and caring. Isn't that what any parent wants?

JOURNAL AND/OR DISCUSSION QUESTIONS

1. What are three rights of the disabled?
2. What did you find most interesting about Maggie Blair's narrative?
3. What are two disabilities you might think of when reading this article?
4. What was the closing statement regarding what Kevin Cooney wanted for his child?
5. How do you suppose you would teach children with different abilities and/or special needs?

Chapter Thirteen

Commentary and Personal Experience

Teaching and "Being" Special Needs

This chapter commences with writing by Patricia Mason, EdD. In her writing she calls attention to identified socio-emotional, academic, and behavioral needs of learners. Then, Marc Hoberman writes about how his epilepsy impacted his childhood, his years in teaching, and his recent retirement.

COMMENTARY: ENGAGING STUDENTS WITH EXCEPTIONALITIES, *PATRICIA MASON, EDD*

Introduction

I am a tenured professor at Molloy College in Rockville Centre, New York. Before that I was a teacher, and before that a person without a title other than *adolescent, child, baby*, or my name. In each of those stages, whether in the school or outside of it, there are exceptionalities/special needs/different abilities in learning. This is realized just by the nature that we're not all the same. We look different from one another, and, as you read in the beginning of this book, recognizing that helps us to understand that we learn differently from one another. And that learning takes place across the curriculum, at any grade level and in any discipline.

"Now"

Presently I teach a course titled, Curriculum Content, Practices and Environmental Issues for Teaching Adolescent Students with Disabilities. I've practiced teaching for decades. I've noticed that a very big factor in successful student achievement is that educators be cognizant of identified socio-emotional, academic, and behavioral needs of learners. These are such that they may interfere with learning demands in both the inclusive and special needs classrooms. However, these factors may be helpful as well.

Teachers can struggle to provide opportunities to support the individual and unique learning needs of younger as well as older students, many of whom can benefit from different and varied teaching strategies. In the aforementioned course, teacher candidates create lessons for future or present adolescent special needs students. Of course, the realization is that while the label of *teenager* is indicative of one's age, it is not necessarily of one's ability level.

Explanation of Graduate Course

The description of this graduate course recognizes the importance of integrating engaging and interactive instruction, as stated in the syllabus: "This course is designed to review curriculum in reading, mathematics, and written composition in grades 7–12. It will enable participants to develop strategies and provide environmental benefits for secondary students challenged to access state curriculum." Simply stated, the strategies and the project and performance-based assignments and lessons need to address the curriculum, but the differentiation of instruction technique enables the learner to digest the material. Subsequently, adaptations are made based on learning differences of the classroom population. The best way to teach that is to model it, I believe.

The teaching and learning that transpires over the semester provides a framework to support teacher candidates and the creation of learning opportunities to meet the academic and learning challenges of adolescents with different abilities and special needs. Subsequently, the course modules outline an approach to engage teacher candidates to develop and practice a variety of teaching strategies across all content areas.

The strategies are specific to meet grade-level content expectations along with presented metacognitive skills. Throughout the course, case studies and accompanying IEPs provide relevant details, which present a variety of examples of students' unmet needs encountered in many classrooms (i.e., learning, attention, and behavioral and motivation differences). The strategies presented also have to take into consideration the clinical information about the disability in each case study. Student profiles in each of these were specifically chosen to help teacher candidates discuss and practice creating techniques with a purpose (engagement, review, or mastery).

Professor Modeling Differentiation and Learner Engagement

In each class session, teacher candidates are encouraged to recognize that many of their adolescent students benefit from engaging prompts. These may be video clips, cartoons from the internet, lyrics from a song, or portions of television commercials. The idea is to captivate the student learner through material that is known and relevant to them.

One strategy that encompasses engagement for our course and serves as modeling differentiation of instruction to meet the student's needs is through use of an interactive wheel. Let me explain: The wheel consists of six to eight spokes that describe various options for students to respond to an instructional objective or a chapter in our textbook. As shown below, students' responses demonstrate their comprehension, application, and evaluation of the lesson's concepts. One section of the wheel is done by a student, a small group, or a partnership.

The activities on the wheel, clockwise, are:

- With a partner, create a graphic organizer for the assigned chapter.
- Use your assigned color marker to write the responses discussed in group on the color-coded chart paper.
- Create and post a three-tier assignment for the class to review. Do this with a partner.
- Work with a student from a different content area to create an alternative assessment and accompanying rubric.
- Share your list of accommodations for the assigned student. Include the objective of the lesson.
- Read the quote. Make two columns. On the right side, identify one word and one sentence you found significant. On the left side, write your reflection on each one.

Review/Evaluation

Toward the end of the semester, students are assigned to bring a sample activity to interchange with those posted on the wheel. This arrangement strategy is a helpful tool because it has multiple purposes: engagement, a measure of participation, and content assessment. After the teacher candidates observe their classmates' positive response to each other's additions to the wheel, the relevance of such a tool is noted for their future classroom practice.

Subsequently, students help students, and practicing this in our course provides the opportunity to carry it over to their own classrooms. Overall, the idea of using the wheel and other active-involvement-style lessons serves as a model for everyone in the class. Personal immersion in learning though varied interactive techniques finds these teacher candidates establishing that their students' learning is not for the parents or the teacher, but for the students themselves.

Closing Comments

In summation, I have used techniques in class to engage learners in lessons so they'll model these for their present or future students. One important reason for doing this is that many students at the adolescent level come to school feeling defeated. Much of this may be because they have not been taught in a way that involves them in the learning experience. A teacher's disposition and pedagogy/teaching techniques can encourage and empower their students to build knowledge, skills, and confidence. Each teacher's use of an interactive approach has its own propose. The purposes include introduction, reinforcement, and construction of knowledge by engaging the students to foster memory. Each one is a building block to successful teaching and learning.

A TEACHER WITH EPILEPSY: FROM CHILDHOOD THROUGH RETIREMENT, *MARC HOBERMAN*

A "Now" Reflection

I have recently retired after a very rewarding thirty-three-year career as a middle school and high school English teacher, and I now reflect on what I believe made me successful in the classroom. Primarily, this would be my experience as a student and adult who was diagnosed with epilepsy at the age of seventeen. Although the diagnosis came in my teen years, the illness actually existed for many years before that.

Personally experiencing special needs, or at least needing different ways of instruction, assisted me in helping children of varied backgrounds, and perhaps I was enabled to comprehend the teaching and learning process from the perspective of someone with ADHD and epilepsy with respect to the socialization in a classroom as much as the academics of that space.

Only two years ago, at the age of fifty-four, did I share my diagnosis with people outside of my immediate family by writing my memoir, *Adversity Defeated: Turn Your Struggles into Strengths*. And I reiterate that although very few people were aware of my illness, I think my personal experiences directly impacted my effectiveness in the classroom. Certainly, being a child with a learning problem influenced my understanding of others with learning differences, regardless of the cause.

The Beginning

In 1974 I was walking home from elementary school with my friend Robbie. I began to babble and stare into space and grew increasingly incoherent. Fortunately, Robbie's father was a doctor, and so Robbie was aware that something was wrong. An hour later, I was found unconscious in the basement of my parents' apartment complex. I was taken to a hospital, and after three days there it was determined that I probably had a virus and had fainted in the building's laundry room. Although my EEG showed irregularities, other medical tests I had taken were perfectly normal.

I was a very active child, and many teachers remarked that I was too active—or even hyperactive. There was no diagnosis of ADD or ADHD fifty years ago, but I am relatively sure I had/have one of those, probably the latter. In these early schooling years, overall, I was able to manage my academics with certain interactive study techniques.

As a youngster, I found that I exemplified the belief of Edgar Dale (1946; 1954; 1969), which I discovered in my early teaching career. His *Cone of Experience*, which was updated two times after its original writing in 1946, related that learners retain more information by what they experience. Today, I think this is referred to as "learning by doing." In earlier parts of this book, Schiering refers to this as "experiential learning." Dale's actual *Cone* relates that individuals remember 10% of what they read, 20% of what they hear, 30% of what they see, 50% of what they see and hear, 70% of what students say or write, and 90% of what they do, as in performing a task.

Basically, I did well in school from kindergarten through sixth grade. When I studied, I was unable to memorize large amounts of information, as rote memorization never really worked for me. But I found that if I role-played the material, I could retain it and own it. If I was engaged in the lesson being presented, I was successful in retaining what was being conveyed.

Teen Years

My education changed drastically around tenth grade. At the beginning of tenth grade, I switched high schools. A tumultuous move from Yonkers, New York, to Hollywood, Florida, found me feeling very alone in my new surroundings. Although my cousins lived nearby, I missed my many friends and classmates from my home. I recall making the "most" of those times.

My cousin Candace and I were preparing to visit her brother at college. He was attending the University of Florida in Gainesville, and we jumped at the chance to join him one weekend. Just fifteen minutes into the trip, I became incoherent while turning onto an exit ramp. Very shortly after, I stiffened up and slammed on the gas. Although I was basically unconscious behind the wheel, my cousin was able to steer my 1977 Mustang through a toll booth and then slam on the brakes.

As it turned out, the incoherent phase of the drive was a petit mal seizure, and I stiffened up as I was in the throes of a grand mal seizure. When I was released from the emergency room of the nearby hospital a few hours later, I had a bottle of antiseizure medication and the diagnosis of epilepsy.

What followed this experience was a two-year ordeal of depression and uncontrolled seizures. I researched my illness for several months, and when we moved back to New York I met a renowned neurologist who was able to keep my seizures pretty much under control. Still, learning was difficult for me. I was focused on how my body was feeling each day and was on constant alert for the next petit mal seizure, which was normally followed by a more severe one.

My grades plummeted in the beginning of high school, and I was no longer motivated to do well. I considered myself unlucky. My parents told all my teachers that I had been diagnosed with epilepsy, but only two spoke to me about it, and it was only a discussion about what they should do if I had a seizure in class. No one ever asked me how I was feeling or how I was dealing with my diagnosis. From this I became acutely aware that school/the classroom is not just a place for academics, but one where we need to look at the whole person. Social cognition is a vital component for students and teachers alike.

A few years later, my grades improved and I learned new study techniques that assisted me in college. I was determined not to let my situation rule or define me. Interestingly, I still kept my illness a secret, and even as a teacher I never disclosed my diagnosis of epilepsy to the outside world. This was a personal choice.

Teaching and Two Different Ways

During my teaching career, I didn't see the need to announce or share that I was an epileptic. However, perhaps because of my condition, I found I was mindful of students' learning difficulties. I thought that I had a special relationship with those in my classes, because I often met them at "their reality." Fundamentally, I became interested in *different ways* of educating the students who were in my classes.

First Example

Since I was aware that seizures often affect one's memory, I researched mnemonic devices and created my own through the years. This transferred over to all my students, not just those who had illnesses or learning disabilities, but also those who didn't. I found that as I learned, I taught, and vice versa. I used this device or technique to make learning more interesting than the implementation of "I tell you this and you listen and try to recall what I said," or students taking notes and referring to them.

Case in point: the word *ephemeral* means "short lived." A girl in my seventh-grade class thought the word was pronounced "F-Meryll." Her word association was that a girl named Meryl received an F on her report card and she was killed. As strange as this association sounds, the student used the word correctly on the vocabulary exam and often used it in essays.

Even though she forced the word into some of her writing, she was always correct with her usage. It was not necessary that I understand the connection; rather, it was important that the correlations and associations made sense to the student. Basically, this mnemonic device—a different way of teaching learning, I've been repeatedly told—was "enjoyable," like an educational game.

Second Example

Another technique I utilized was word association or visualization, which is known as stacking. I incorporated this into lessons to enhance memory and the ability to recall information. An example would be to recall the chronological order in which the first thirteen colonies became states. If you place a piece of cracked *chinaware* on the floor and a *pen* is stacked in the crack and a *Jersey* cow is balanced on top of the pen and King *George* sits on the cow . . . you are stacking the information and seeing it in your mind's eye. Or you could make cutouts of these objects and put one on top of the other for a more kinesthetic approach. Nonetheless, using the aforementioned visualization, I would list the first four colonies as:

1. China*ware* = Dela*ware*
2. *Pen* = *Penn*sylvania
3. *Jersey* cow = New *Jersey*
4. King *George* = *Georg*ia

Of course, the list goes on, covering all thirteen colonies in a unique and fun manner that can be easily retrieved for instant recall. While this is a way for special needs or different abilities students to gain knowledge, I found stacking also works well with otherwise unmotivated students because it is not the usual way they learn or study. Bottom line: this educational word game put learning in their hands, figuratively and/or literally, depending on the modality/modalities selected for representing those thirteen colonies.

Before Retirement and Afterward

Experiential learning has continually been at the forefront of my educational strategies, and I have used numerous differentiated instructional techniques.

As the years have transpired, I call attention to my repeatedly keeping my students' different abilities in mind. Their socialization in the classroom has also been a matter of importance, along with success in their academics. I have worked at making lessons that would create interest while students were fully engaged in obtaining information for retention of it.

Students come into our classroom, often, it seems, randomly assigned. I believe it's important to know that young people bring many struggles with them to school each day. These are present in all classrooms, regardless of where one teaches. I am a proponent of differentiated instruction, and simultaneously, I am also mindful of the necessity to connect with students by having conversations with them and using methods that meet their needs. This is in opposition to lecturing or continual direct instruction, which I think is no longer effective in present-day education.

When my memoir was published, two years before I retired, I was amazed at how accepting the students were. Even as an adult, I felt there was a stigma attached to my epilepsy, and I kept it to myself. In hindsight, I think that this was a mistake. My last two years teaching were, by far, my most rewarding. Students opened up to me even more about their illnesses and struggles, and the level of trust that was always present in my teaching career grew tenfold.

Before retirement and now after it, I became CEO of Grade Success Education, a full-service tutoring business. I combine word association and visualization to help students learn and memorize information. I use different ways of instruction to meet the needs of those who seek out this instructional service. In the long run, as I previously stated, teaching is not just about academics. Teaching is about delivering instruction in a manner that can be accepted by students and addresses their need for differentiation. What I keep in mind is that we are all unique individuals, and the different ways we teach paves the pathway for a successful learning environment.

JOURNAL AND/OR DISCUSSION QUESTIONS

1. What are two of Patricia Mason's ideas regarding learner engagement and modeling differentiation?
2. What were two experiences Marc Hoberman had that, in your opinion, impacted his learning and teaching? And what is one way he implemented his experience with respect to his teaching?

Chapter Fourteen

Author's Summative Sharing

Classroom Comfort Zone

At the start of this book, you were invited to examine the content. Later, you were invited to analyze the premises of how to reach and teach varied learners. Information about Response to Intervention and Individualized Education Programs was given, and other chapters addressed processing style and creating memories. The reciprocity of thinking was examined, and combining thinking and feelings was given attention. Personal commentaries of teachers, professors, and parents working with their student learners or their children provided a personal view of special needs and different abilities. If breaking this down, one might say that the book has succinctly addressed:

1. Means to educate all students, not just for the sake of educating or passing a test, but mainly for each one to enjoy learning;
2. Creating memory by providing experiences in which the students could be involved, or totally immersed; the mode of instruction was agreeable to the student; and the teacher modeling was in alignment with instructional techniques as well as with a pleasant demeanor;
3. How IM learning techniques engage learners and are accomplished through varied forms of instruction (IM's IBR, ABLCs, and P/PBL) to address the way students best learn, as well as achieve and retain information;
4. Creating a classroom environment that is conducive to learning because there continually is a feeling of comfort when being there.

AUTHOR'S PHILOSOPHIES: A NARRATIVE

As individuals we each have different abilities and sometimes special needs. These may be in the social arena or in the academic one. Perhaps they are in both sectors. Regardless, each requires variation of instruction to meet the needs of each person. When students' requirements are met, as this book relates, by using interactive instructional resources, the learner *remembers the experience*. Yes, *experiential learning* is the operative term. For example, project/performance-based learning allows for personal involvement and for retention of material through that involvement, regardless of the subject area, age, or grade level of the learner.

We reflect most effectively on brain-based and motor memory, as well as the emotional involvement in a lesson that results from the experiences of it. These three factors solidify the acquisition, orientation, decision making, and problem solving involved in the act of remembering. This is so much so that often what we think and feel becomes what we say and do.

And, as one reviews the material in this book, especially the chapters addressing identifying and implementing what one is thinking, one realizes that we learn and teach simultaneously and that we're all teachers of something. Primarily that "something" is one's demeanor. The way an individual acts is a representation of that person's character.

COMFORT ZONE

Item four in the the list that begins this chapter addresses the classroom as a comfort zone. Perhaps that is the very essence of this book and its companion. Perhaps that is the essence of all teaching: to create a space where learners feel at ease and want to challenge themselves, take in information until it becomes knowledge, and ultimately to share this knowledge with someone else who is a learner, whether in a school setting or outside it.

For me, in achieving that comfort zone, it is not just the academic IM and its components that are important, but the social cognition factor invoved with having conversation *with* others; self- and classmate-appreciation is vital. And instructional techniques that involve the learner in self-efficacy with social interaction provide valuable opportunities for successes that are personal as well as academic. The idea that these two factors meld together smoothly is the heart of the matter for learning, regardless of one's abilities or classifications.

That sense of well-being, fostered by sharing in a way that one feels enabled and engaged, makes for a community of learning. As you know by now, the IM is about how to create such a community. This space is where those present identify cooperation and collaboration as mainstays in being "fair": fair about having different abilities and ways that one processes information, and addressing those abilities. The definition of *fair* is not everyone getting the same thing, or getting what they may want, but instead it is everyone getting what is needed.

Reflecting back to the mid-1970s, I originated an idea about how to create a classroom community of caring with the IM and its components, as well as socialization of a viable nature. This was accomplished through my ongoing *enactment* of the "No put-downs . . . only lift-ups!" statement. What this entailed was acceptance of individuals' work and efforts to do assignments, and acceptance of oneself as well. Subsequently, praise, as opposed to negative comments, were the norm.

If there was something that appeared grossly out of place, then it would be addressed, not in front of the class, but privately, with suggestions about how the next assignment might be done. There were not demands about how to correct or an imposition of the idea of "failure" onto the individual. "To what end," I thought would lead a learner: "If there is positivity in the classroom, then one might take it on as a way to conduct him- or herself." "Only lift-ups" became one classroom rule. And it worked. It took time, but it worked. The comfort zone was created.

A LIFE LESSON

In the late 1990s, my son addressed my St. John's University doctoral candidate class. At the culmination of his talk about what it was like to go from his sense of being a failure at most everything to achieving success, he was asked by one teacher in the course what made him stop being a failure. He replied, "My first success, because once you have the first one you may have as many as you choose to have."

Another class member inquired as to how teachers could get students to "respect" them? He replied, "How do I give you what I don't have for myself? You can only give to another that which you have first for you." His belief was that if you're negative with yourself, then that is how you'll likely be with others. But if you have self-respect and positivity, then you can give that to anyone.

To illustrate his point, he asked the teacher to ask him for an apple. The teacher did that, and he responded that he couldn't give her the apple because he didn't have one. Then he explained that we think in terms of material objects when one asks to have or borrow something, and you can only give that object if you have it to give. "The same thing goes for character traits," he continued. "If I have self-respect, caring, interest, etc., in me, then I can give it to you."

Subsequently, I present the idea of imposing your conscious will to be affirmative with yourself and those you know. Then you can experience not putting others down, but lifting them up through your words and behaviors. You can do this for yourself as well through positive self-talk. One thing is for sure: You must rely upon yourself to institute the methods and ideas for interactive learning in the classroom brought forth in this book.

You are the change agent or promoter of different ways for different abilities. You are the one on whom implementation of this book's content depends. You are the one to create the classroom comfort zone and bring it to those in that shared-environment. You accomplish this with lessons designed to involve the learner and valuing caring, responsibility, fairness, trustworthiness, respect, and kindness while possessing and demonstrating, overall, good will.

In summation: all the ideas presented in the pages of this book are about promoting personal involvement through self-acceptance. By so doing, in using the Interactive Method and its components, addressed as "different ways" of instruction, for the promotion of self-worth, the valuation that one can be successful academically and socially is realized. The comments from those personally involved in use of variable ways of instruction for the "personal touch" of this book are certainly a valuable guide for social cognition.

Finally, the statements that close this writing come to relate the concepts of we are the caretakers of other people's children, regardless of the grade level we teach. We may identify special needs with the idea of interactive learning for children with different abilities and provide instruction in different ways to accommodate the students in our classroom. As one embraces/holds onto these concepts—whether as teacher or learner---one comes to the perception of "You and I are enough." The ownership of those words results in personal and whole-class empowerment, and most importantly, individual self-acceptance and reliance. With that one can achieve beyond measure!

JOURNAL AND/OR DISCUSSION QUESTIONS

1. What chapter did you most like in this book and why did you make that choice?
2. What is meant by the term *personal touch*?
3. What does it mean to be a *change agent*?
4. What are three perspectives you have on special needs, different abilities, and different ways of learning?
5. Who qualifies as having special needs and/or different abilities, as presented in this book? What are some thoughts, ideas, opinions, judgments, or feelings you have about those categories?

References

Abedi, J., & O'Neil, H. F. (1996) Reliability and validity of a state metacognitive inventory: Potential for alternative assessment. *Journal of Educational Research*, *89*(4), 234–45.

Abourafeh, D. A. (2018a). *One way does not fit all.* (Unpublished). Rebecca Center for Music Therapy, Molloy College, Rockville Centre, NY.

Abourafeh, D. A. (2018b). *A phenomenological inquiry into an autistic adolescent's experience in relationship-based music therapy from the perspectives of the adolescent and parent* (Unpublished master's thesis). Molloy College, Rockville Centre, NY.

American Institute for Learning and Human Development. (n.d.). 8 Principles of Neurodiversity. http://www.institute4learning.com/resources/articles/neurodiversity/

Americans with Disability Act (ADA). (2009). *A Guide to Disability Rights.*

Andale, H. G. (2000). Using rubrics to promote thinking and learning. *Educational Leadership*, *57*(5), http://www.ascd.org/publications/educational-leadership/feb00/v0157/num05/Using-Rubrics-to-Promote-Thinking-and-Learning

Armstrong, T. (1995). *The myth of the ADD child: 50 ways to improve your child's behavior and attention span without labels, drugs, or coercion.* New York, NY: Penguin Random House.

———. (2011). *The power of neurodiversity: Unleashing the advantages of your differently wired brain.* Cambridge, MA: DaCapo Lifelong/Perseus Books.

———. (2012). *Neurodiversity in the classroom: Strength-based strategies to help students with special needs succeed in school and life.* Alexandria, VA: ASCD.

———. (2017, April). Neurodiversity: The future of special education. *Educational Leadership*, *74*(7), 10–16.

Blair, M. (2018). *Disabilities, differences and diversity: College course syllabus* (Graduate). EDU5240.01 Diverse abilities and needs. Rockville Centre, NY. Molloy College.

Bodrova, E., & Leong, D. (2007). *Tools of the mind: The Vygotskian approach to early childhood education* (2nd ed.). Upper Saddle River, NJ: Pearson.

Bogner, D. (2011). Tasks for the teacher. In M. S. Schiering, D. Bogner, & J. Buli-Holmberg (Eds.), *Teaching and learning: A model for academic and social cognition.* Lanham, MD. Rowman & Littlefield.

Bogner, D., & Schiering, M. (2007). Definition of feelings as "root responses" to stimuli. in *Brain World: Humanity's New Frontier*, *4*(2), Canada. IBREA and portion of course syllabus. Rockville Centre, NY: Molloy College.

Brandt, R. (1999). Educators need to know about the human brain. *Phi Delta Kappan*, *81*(3), 235–38.

Bruscia, K. E. (1987). *Improvisational models of music therapy* . Springfield, IL: Charles C. Thomas.

Calder, M. (2017). *Thinking skills application.* Rhame Avenue School principal (Retired). E. Rockaway, NY.

Carpente, J. (2016). Investigating the effectiveness of a developmental, individual difference, relationship-based (DIR) improvisational music therapy program on social communication for children with ASD. *Music Therapy Perspectives, 35*(2), 160–74.

Cooney, K. (2018). Autism awareness: Interviewing a different abilities child's parent. (Unpublished). A presentation for Molloy's Circle K (CKI) College version of the Kiwanis Club. Molloy College. Rockville Centre, NY.

Dale, E. (1969). *Cone of experience: Audio-visual methods in teaching* (3rd ed.). New York, NY: Holt, Rinehart & Winston.

Deaf Linx. (n.d.). Retrieved from http://www.deaflinx.com.

Delialioglu, O. (2012). Student engagement in blended learning. *Journal of Educational Technology and Society, 10*(2), 133–46.

Dewey, J. (1945). Self-realization as the moral ideal. In *John Dewey: The early works, 1882–1924* (vol. 4). Carbondale, IL: Southern Illinois Press.

Dunn, R. (1995). *Possible behavioral characteristics of special needs students.* Professor published handout on An introduction to learning styles. Handout for course on adjusting teaching methods to student needs. St. John's University Cohort 1, Sparkill, NY.

———. (1996). Author's notes from: Learning Styles doctorate course. St. John's Univ. Queens, NY.

Dunn R., & Dunn, K. (1976; 1992). *The Dunn and Dunn Learning Style Model* (1st and 4th ed.). Englewood Cliffs, NJ: Prentice Hall.

———. (1978). *Teaching students through their learning styles: A practical approach.* Englewood Cliffs, NJ: Prentice Hall.

Eckardt, P., & Craig, M. (Unpublished). Special Needs Different Abilities Deferent Ways: A reflection on diversity of colleagues teaching methods. Molloy College. Rockville Centre, NY.

Edudemic (2015). Every teacher's guide to assessment. www.edudemic.com/summative-and-formative-assessments.

Eide, B., & Eide, F. (2011). *The dyslexic advantage: Unlocking the hidden potential of the dyslexic brain.* New York, NY: Penguin.

Garcia, M. (2012). Creative cognition. *Brain World: Humanity's New Frontier Magazine, 3*(4), 56.

Glatthorn, A. (1995). *Developing the classroom curriculum: Developing a quality curriculum.* Alexandria, VA: ASCD.

Goddard, Y. L., Goddard, R. D., & Tschannen-Moran, M. (2007). A theoretical and empirical investigation of teacher collaboration for school improvement and student achievement in public elementary schools. *Teachers College Record, 109*, 877–96.

Heide, G. A. (2000). Using rubrics to promote thinking and learning. *Educational Leadership, 57*(5), 13–18.

Greenspan, S. I., & Wieder, S. (2009). *Engaging autism: Using the floor time approach to help children relate, communicate, and think* . Cambridge, MA: Da Capo Press.

Groce, Nora Ellen. (1985). *Everyone here spoke sign language: Hereditary deafness on Martha's Vineyard.* Cambridge, MA: Harvard University Press.

Hoberman, M. (2016). *Adversity defeated: Turn your struggles into strengths.* Monsey, NY: Grade Success Publishing.

———. (2018). A parent and educator's perspectives on a learner with dyslexia. Monsey, NY: Grade Success Publishing.

Hunter, M. (1989). Quotation on different learning preferences. In R. E. Salvin. On mastery learning and mastery teaching. *The Association for Supervision and Curriculum and Development.* Alexandria, Virginia.

Individuals with Disabilities Education Act (IDEA). (1990). Part 300.8 (a) (1). Changes to language of the law regarding putting the person first. P.L.94-142 Appendix F to part 300-Index for IDEA-Part B (34 CFR Part 300). https: //stics.ed.gov/ IDEA/regs/b/d/300.304/b/3.

———. (2004). Part 300.8(a)(1). Appendix F to Part 300—Index for IDEA—Part B (34 CFR Part 300). Retrieved fromhttps://sites.ed.gov/idea/regs/b/d/300.304/b/3.

Individuals with Disability Education Act (IDEA) Reauthorizations. (1997, 2004).

Introduction to Contemporary Special Education: New Horizons, 2014.

Jaarsma, P., & Welin, S. (2012). Autism as a natural human variation: Reflections on the claims of the neurodiversity movement. *Health Care Analysis, 20*(1), 20–30.

Keefe, J. W. (Ed.). (1979). *Learning styles: An overview, The student learning styles: Diagnosing and prescribing programs.* Reston, VA: National Association of Secondary School Principals.

Keefe, J. W., & Languis, M. (1983). Description of the learning style profile. In J. W. Keefe and J. S. Monk (Eds.), *NASSP Bulletin* (pp. 43–53). Reston, VA: National Association of Secondary School Principals.

Kelly, M. (2017). Defining project and performance based learning. www.ThoughtCo.com

Laupheimer, L. (2016). Enjoyment of interactive learning. In M. Schiering (Ed.), *Learning and teaching creative cognition: The interactive book report.* Lanham, MD: Rowman & Littlefield

Maheshwari, S. (2016) You Tube video of Edgar Dale's *Cone of Experience.* http://www.vkmaheshwari.com/WP/?p=2332

Marsala, N. (2018). *Which superhero do I want to be? Superhero selection.* Decision Making Graphic Organizer. Integrated ELA and Reading; EDU. 506A. Molloy College, Rockville Centre, NY.

Mason. P. (2018). Engaging Students with Exceptionalities. Molloy College, Rockville Centre, NY.

McTighe, J., & Wiggins, G. (1999). *Understanding by design handbook.* Alexandria, VA: Association for Supervision and Curriculum Development.

Moroney, R. (2017). *Comments on receiving and interpreting information.* Molloy College Division of Education. Rockville Centre, NY.

National Association for Gifted Children. (NAGC; n.d.). "Twice Exceptional Students." Retrieved from https://nagc.org/resources-publications/resources-parents/twice-exceptional-students.

National Center on Response to Intervention. (2018). Tier 1: High-Quality Classroom Instruction, Screening, and Group Interventions. p.1. http://rtinetwork.org/learn/what/whatisrti

National Institute of Child Health and Development (NICHD). (n.d.). Retrieved from http://nichd.nih.gov.

Nordoff, P., & Robbins, C. (2007). *Creative music therapy: A guide to fostering clinical musicianship* (2nd Ed.). Gilsum, NH: Barcelona.

Olsen, D. G. (1995). "Less" can be "more" in the promotion of thinking. *Social Education,* 59(3), 130–38.

Redondo, J. (2018) *Careers path options: My five-year career choice, fireman, teacher/professor, law enforcement.* Decision Making Graphic Organizer. Integrated ELA and Reading; EDU. 506A. Molloy College, Rockville Centre, NY.

Robertson, S. M. (2009). Neurodiversity, quality of life, and autistic adults: Shifting research and professional focuses onto real-life challenges. *Disability Studies Quarterly, 30*(1), 27. http://dsq-sds.org/article/view/1069/1234

Ryley, T. (2018). *From the heart: Having different abilities children: Their dad's narrative.* Essay for Project SAVE and Dignity for all students' act. Molloy College. Rockville Centre, NY.

RTI Action Network. (2018). What is RTI? Retrieved from www.rtinetwork.org/learn/what.

Schiering, J. (2017). *Special education: A resource room teacher's views.* Professional opinion regarding paper. Manch Elementary School. Las Vegas, Nevada.

Schiering, M. R. (2015). Qualities of a leader, from LinkedIn "Princess bride" leadership lessons. In M. S. Schiering (Ed.). *Learning and teaching creative cognition: The interactive book report* (pp 51–58). Lanham, MD: Rowman & Littlefield.

———. (1984). A Day in Ancient Egypt. Social Studies year's syllabus Exxon's Impact II: Creativity in the Classroom Award. Farley Middle School. Stony Point, NY.

———. (1996). Making the IBR: Directions for classroom implementation Stony Point Elementary School. Stony Point, NY.

———. (1998). *Our interactive earth-day book.* NYS Earth-day completion, Albany, NY.

———. (1999a). *Evolving from cognition to metacognition* became *The reciprocal thinking phases: Cognition and metacognition* in 2011. (Doctoral dissertation.) St. John's University. Queens, NY, and Molloy College. Rockville Centre, NY.

———. (1999b). The effects of learning-style instructional resources on fifth grade suburban students' metacognition, achievement, attitudes, and ability to teach themselves (EdD dissertation). St. John's University. Queens, NY.

———. (2000-present). *NYS Project SAVE (Safe schools against violence in education)* and *What's right with you: An interactive character development guide*. Lanham, MD: Rowman & Littlefield.

———. (2014–present). Dignity for All Student Act (DASA) Workshops, slides 28 and 30. Rockville Centre, NY: Molloy College.

———. (2003). The "how"and "who" of teaching and learning. In Raynor and Armstrong, et al. (Eds.), *Bridging Theory and Practice*. ELSIN 8th International European Learning Styles Conference, Hull, UK.

———. (2011, Summer). "I think therefore I am; I feel therefore I am: Cognition and emotion of the brain and mind." In *Brain World: Humaity's New Frontier*, 4(2), 52.

———. (2014). Character trait role-play. In *Teaching critical and creative thinking: An interactive workbook*. Lanham, MD: Rowman & Littlefield.

———. (2015). *Learning and teaching creative cognition: The interactive book report*. Lanham, MD: Rowman & Littlefield.

———. (2016a). *Learning and teaching creative cognition: The interactive book report*. Lanham, MD: Rowman & Littlefield.

———. (2016b). Geometric shapes: A math word problem floor game. In *Teaching critical and creative thinking: An interactive workbook*. Lanham, MD: Rowman & Littlefield.

———. (2016c). *Teaching creative and critical thinking: An interactive workbook*. Lanham, MD: Rowman & Littlefield.

———. (2017). *What's right with you: An interactive character development guide*. Lanham, MD: Rowman & Littlefield.

———. (2018). Contemporary issues in education: Character education and development. p. 273. In J. F. Marino and M. S. Russo (ed.), *The Philosophy of Education* (2nd ed.), p. 273. New York: SophiaOmni Publications.

Schering, M. S., & Bogner, D. (2008). Definitions of thoughts, ideas, opinions, judgments and feelings. EDU. 506A: Integrated ELA and reading course syllabus addendum. p. 7. Rockville Centre, NY: Molloy College.

———. (2011). Definitions of thoughts, ideas, opinions, judgments and feelings. In M. S. Schiering, D. Bogner, & J. Buli-Holmberg (Eds.), *Teaching and learning: A model for academic and social cognition*. Lanham, MD: Rowman & Littlefield.

Schiering, M. S., Bogner, D., & Buli-Holmberg, J. (Eds.). (2011). *Teaching and larning: A model for academic and social cognition*. Lanham, MD. Rowman & Littlefield.

Schiering, M., & Byrne, J. (2016). The linear process of creativity. In M. Schiering (Ed.), *Teaching creative and critical thinking: An interactive workbook*. Lanham, MD: Rowman & Littlefield.

Schiering, M. S., & Dunn, K. (2001). Student empowerment: from cognition to metacognition. In R. Dunn (Ed.), *The art of significantly increasing science achievement test scores: Research and practical applications*. New York: St. John's University Press, Center for the Study of Learning and Teaching Styles.

Schiering, M. S., & Marino, A. (2016). Reciprocal process of creativity. In M. Schiering (Ed.), *Teaching creative and critical thinking: An interactive workbook*. Lanham, MD: Rowman & Littlefield.

Schon, D. (1997). Reflective practice and professional development. ERIC Digest. Retrieved from http: //eric.ed.gov/.

Silberman, S. (2015). *NeuroTribes: The legacy of autism and the future of neurodiversity*. New York, NY: Avery.

Sorel, S. (2004). *Presenting Carly and Elliot: Exploring roles and relationships in a motherson dyad in Nordoff -Robbins music therapy* . (Unpublished doctoral dissertation). New York University, New York, NY.

———. (2010). Presenting Carly and Elliot: Exploring roles and relationships in a mother-son dyad in Nordoff-Robbins music therapy. *Qualitative Inquiries in Music Therapy, 5*, 173–238.

Sousa, D., & Tomlinson, C. (2018). *Differentiation and the brain: How neuroscience supports the learner-friendly classroom* (2nd ed.). Bloomington, IN: Solution Tree Press.

Spotkov, L. (2014). *Thoughts on using self-corrective instruction*. An IBR Activity. Integrated ELA and Reading; EDU.506A. Molloy College, Rockville Centre, NY.

Sullivan, A. (2008). 16 learning disabilities with definitions: Information for Teachers Thiells Elementary School. Thiells, NY.

The Education for All Handicapped Children Act. (1975). https://www.govinfo.gov/content/pkg/STATUTE-89/pdf/STATUTE-89-Pg773.pdf

Thompson, G., & McFerran, K. S. (2015). "We've got a special connection": Qualitative analysis of descriptions of change in the parent–child relationship by mothers of young children with ASD. *Nordic Journal of Music Therapy, 24* (1), 3–26.

Tobias, S., & Everson, H. T. (1995, April). *Development and validation of an objective measure of metacognition appropriate for group administration*. Paper presented at a symposium on "Issues in Metacognitive Research and Assessment," at the annual convention of the American Educational Research Association, San Francisco, CA.

Tomlinson, C. A. (1995). *How to differentiate instruction in a mixed ability classroom*. Alexandria, VA: ASCD.

Tomlinson, C. A., & Allan, S. (2000). *Leadership for differentiating schools and classrooms*. Alexandria, VA: ASCD.

Tschannen, M., & Woolfolk H. (2007). The differential antecedents of self-efficacy beliefs of novice and experienced teachers. *Teaching and Teacher Education, 23*, 944–56.

U.S. Office of Education. (1968). First annual report of the national advisory committee on handicapped children. Washington, DC: US Department of Health Education and Welfare.

Warren, P., & Nugent, N. (2010). The Music Connections Programmed: Parents' perceptions of their children's involvement in music therapy. *New Zealand Journal of Music Therapy, 8*, 8–33.

Webster's II New Riverside Dictionary (1996). Revised Edition, Office Edition. Boston, MA: Houghton Mifflin.

About the Author

Reverend Dr. **Marjorie S. Schiering** has devoted her career as an educator to the concept of student learners having a sense of self-efficacy, reliance, and empowerment. This is considered to be a direct result of the implementation and application of her experience-based Interactive Method (IM) of teaching and learning. Beginning in an inner-city school in Columbus, Ohio, and then taking these ideas to North Carolina and upstate New York, she honed her concepts to include the teaching of thinking.

Dr. S., as she prefers to be professionally addressed, received her bachelor's degree in childhood education from The Ohio State University and earned her master's degree in reading from the College of New Rochelle in New York. Her doctoral work, in instructional leadership, was done at St. John's University. She wholeheartedly supports the concept of teaching students the way they best learn, along with their active involvement in the learning process.

Dr. S. has presented extensively and published on the use of the IM with the Interactive Book Report book and workbook addressing critical and creative thinking. In 2003 she developed a model for academic and social cognition and coauthored a book, which led to presentations on that model. She has also presented in the United States and abroad on the topics of character development (*What's Right with You*, 2016), children's literature, and the idea of one being "enough" coinciding with her behavioral "No Put Downs . . . Only Lift Ups" philosophy. These presentations were primarily in the United States, England, Norway, Latvia, the Republic of Georgia, and South America.

Brain-based education, with emphasis on engaging the imagination for the purpose of developing and enhancing creativity and critical thinking, has been a mainstay of her teaching endeavors. This has been accompanied by motivating teachers and students, inspiring learners to address their abilities, and creating a safe and positive classroom where there's a true sense of community.

Dr. S. is an ordained interfaith minister and served ten years as a volunteer chaplain at Westchester Medical Center in Valhalla, New York. For the past five years she has been the adviser to Molloy's Circle-K Club, which is a subsidiary of the International Kiwanis Club. She has presented at its statewide NYSpeaking Conference many times and continues to serve her community when called upon to promote positive thinking and human development for a sense of belonging where one lives and/or works.

www.ingramcontent.com/pod-product-compliance
Lightning Source LLC
Chambersburg PA
CBHW030142240426
43672CB00005B/228